9703

D0926458

Treating Perpetrators
of Sexual Abuse

Treating Perpetrators of Sexual Abuse

Sandra L. Ingersoll

Susan O. Patton

Lexington Books

D.C. Heath and Company/Lexington, Massachusetts/Toronto

Library of Congress Cataloging-in-Publication Data
Ingersoll, Sandra L.
    Treating perpetrators of sexual abuse / by Sandra L. Ingersoll and
Susan O. Patton.
        p.   cm.
    ISBN 0-669-21785-9 (alk. paper)
    1. Sex offenders—Rehabilitation—United States.   2. Social work
with criminals—United States.   I. Patton, Susan O.   II. Title.
HQ72.U53I54   1990
364.1′53—dc20   90-5473
                                                                                 CIP

Published simultaneously in Canada
Printed in the United States of America
Casebound International Standard Book Number: 0-669-21785-9
Library of Congress Catalog Card Number: 90-5473

The paper used in this publication meets the minimum requirements of
American National Standard for Information Sciences—Permanence of
Paper for Printed Library Materials, ANSI Z39.48-1984. ∞™

Year and number of this printing:

90 91 92 10 9 8 7 6 5 4 3 2 1

Dedication

This book is dedicated to the thinkers who inspired us, the clients who taught us, the families who supported us through the process, and to each other for the love, strength, and inspiration we have exchanged along the way.

Contents

Figures

Introduction

The perpetration of sexual abuse against children is a growing problem in our society, with many unanswered questions and unaddressed issues. Although we are all pioneers in the field, and few "experts" have emerged, progress and positive outcomes in the treatment of perpetrators are occurring. This book is designed to address the issues faced by every human service worker intervening with perpetrators of sexual abuse. We have attempted to write this book on a practical, clinical level: a "how-to" guide to working with perpetrators of incest and incest-like offenses. We have reviewed literature, worked in the field, and drawn our own conclusions. Basically, we intend for this book to provide information that is practical and useful when you, the worker, are confronted with an incestuous situation. With adaptation, the principles set forth in this book can be applied to other abusive situations, physical, emotional, and even substance abusive families. But within the scope of this book and of our experience, we will deal specifically with incestuous family situations.

This book will be useful for human service workers, such as teachers, nurses, clergy, caseworkers, counselors, judges, therapists, physicians, social workers, law enforcement officers, counselors at law, probation and parole officers, child protection workers, crisis workers, school personnel, prison counselors and administrators, policy makers, planners, program designers, and concerned lay people. We hope our message will become a catalyst, opening the way for constructive and productive changes in the ways we approach the assessment, treatment, and adjudication of perpetrators and their families. We encourage you to take from it a fresh orientation toward comprehensive intervention, relearning, healing, forgiveness, and reshaping lives as opposed to punishment, humiliation, compounded shame, and reoffense. In recent decades, our society has opened enumerable closet doors in the name of individual freedom, humanism, and increased social awareness. We can think of no open door more likely than this one to promote the safety, healing, and wholeness of individuals, families, and generations of families.

In addition, we intend to speak to the issue of treating the perpetrator

and the entire family constellation as a means of protecting the already victimized child as well as the potential victim. We want to see an end to sexual
abuse. This book is a demonstration of our willingness to take a step forward
toward finding intervention points in the complex cycle that perpetuates sexual abuse. We implore you to help us move further still: to use those techniques that fit your style of working, to find ways to empirically test their
effectiveness, to build on our collective knowledge-base and advocate for judicial reform and for development of new and improved treatment programs
for perpetrators, victims, and nonvictimized family members, to find new
ways to promote individual healing, and to seek the best possible means of
protecting victims and potential victims.

There is so much to do. We hope to inspire some readers to join us in
our effort to protect victims and to help perpetrators extricate themselves
from the cycle of abuse.

1
Getting Started

Is Treating the Victim Enough?

As professionals, human service workers are willing to settle for no less than full healing and recovery for the child victim of sexual abuse. Yet, traditionally, we have been satisfied with treating the child victim alone, neglecting the fact that the perpetrator is often a part of that child's family and emotional history for *life*. In this book, we take the position that the *entire family* needs treatment in order to restore it to a functional condition. When family restoration is impossible, however, treating the family systemically can help relationships to heal to an extent where forgiveness and healthful movement beyond the abuse and identification with the abusive relationship can take place. This book's purpose is to help the human service worker attain footing in the relatively uncharted field of treating the perpetrator of sexual abuse.

There has been considerable speculation that victims of sexual abuse, experience victimization in three ways: the initial sexual victimization, the report and its aftermath, and the residual guilt that the victims internalize. Some human service workers feel that by treating only the victims and sparing them the compound pain involved in continuing to deal with the perpetrators, they are confining the damage. As much as we would like to see total healing take place for those victimized, we feel that complete healing can occur only when the perpetrators are able to assume full responsibility for their behavior and to communicate that to the child victims, thus relieving the children of culpability. It would be naïve to equate healing with forgetting; it seems impossible to expect a child who has been sexually abused by a trusted adult to forget that experience. It is possible, however, to work toward a point where the emotional impact of the abusive event is placed into a manageable life context, rather than being allowed to dominate or define the victim's life. The objective in working toward healing is to work through the experience with both the victim and the perpetrator in order to resolve the emotional residue of the experience to the extent that both victim and perpetrator are able to say, "Yes, it happened, and it was horrible, but I am not limited to defining myself or my life in terms of that trauma. I have learned from it and I am able to move on."

What might happen if treatment is terminated before the healing process is complete? Indications from the literature on perpetuation of incestuous sexual abuse from one generation to the next suggest several courses of patterned behavior. The victims are left with the internalized sense that something is "wrong" with them, that they are basically unlovable (otherwise, why would this have happened?). That attitude will be carried into adult relationships, where they may set themselves up for the same kind of patterned abuse experienced in childhood. Furthermore, they may abuse their children as a learned response to the parenting style adapted from their upbringing. They may become sexually promiscuous, turn to drugs or alcohol or self-mutilate. The possible effects of childhood sexual abuse are well-documented elsewhere in the literature. See especially the work of Suzanne Sgroi. For the perpetrators, incomplete healing can set the stage for alienation from family, community, and profession, continued destruction of self-esteem, and most important continued abuse with other victims. Take, for example, the case of Christine:

> Christine had been sexually abused by her uncle between her eighth and eleventh years. She is now twenty-eight and the mother of three children. When her oldest child (male) turned eight years old, she found herself disliking him and becoming very punitive with him. Up to that point, Christine had been a very loving and supportive parent. When she came to me for counseling she was extremely distressed and could not understand what was happening in her relationship with her son. After looking into her own childhood, the abusive history with her uncle surfaced, along with sixteen years of unresolved hurt and rage. Unfortunately, Christine's uncle had died and was unavailable for her to confront. After working on victimization issues, Christine still had unresolved questions: "Why did he choose me?" "Did he hate me?" "Was I an inappropriately sexy child?" Coincidentally, Robert was also in therapy with me—a perpetrator who was unable to work therapeutically with his own child because a court order prevented contact. After thoughtful planning and thorough preparation, and after obtaining written consent from Robert, I asked Christine if she would like to meet with Robert and work through her unresolved issues with him in place of her uncle. She agreed to try it. In therapy, she role-played herself as a child while Robert role-played her uncle. The resulting therapeutic movement made by both Christine and Robert was impressive: they both cried spontaneously and unashamedly during the role-play. (Although effective in this case, this situation should not be replicated unless appropriate consideration for the treatment of the victim warrants such an emotionally charged technique.)

In the case cited, both Christine and Robert found an opportunity for healing that otherwise might not have been available to them. The confrontation was as valuable to Robert as it was to Christine; it was the first time Robert was able to confront the effect of his abusive behavior on his own child. But such opportunities are rare.

The prevailing popular opinion about dealing therapeutically with perpetrators seems to be, "Lock him up and throw the key away!" What we fail to realize when we take that position is that our judicial system does not provide for perpetual punishment for this type of crime. Sooner or later the perpetrator will be out of confinement and back on the streets—usually without having been treated at all. What then? Will there be another victim?

The Perpetuation of Abuse: A Bi-Directional Poison

Research is now confirming that the cycle of victimization is bi-directional, making it even more insidious than we had known. (See figure 1–1 for the Bi-Directional Cycle of Victimization.) In the first generation (we have arbitrarily chosen an intergenerational starting point and labeled it "Generation 1"), a parent abuses a child. In the second generation, the child grows up, becomes a parent, and in turn, abuses a child. The pattern repeats in the third generation. Yet at the same time as the abuse is perpetuated *forward* from generation to generation, it is also being perpetuated *backward*. The parent of Generation 1 is reaching the frail elderly stage of life by the time Generation 3 is established. It may even be the case that by Generation 3, the parent of Generation 1 is unable to live unassisted and may be living with or largely dependent upon the parent of Generation 2. Under the pressures inherent in being the middle generation of the three, this parent, whose offspring have finally become independent (Generation 3), becomes encumbered with an elderly parent (Generation 1). This Generation 2 parent (who was an abused child) is likely to cope with the pressures of dealing with the elderly parent in a similar way to which he or she coped with the pressures of dealing with the Generation 3 child—with abusive behavior. So, we have a two-way cycle: the forward progression of perpetuation of child abuse, and the backward progression of perpetuation of elder abuse.

How do we intervene in this bi-directional cycle of abuse? We believe that intervention is required at many points in the cycle, but in order to arrest the bi-directional nature of the cycle, it is not enough to intervene only with the child victim. We know now that there may be another victim in the other direction, one who is equally vulnerable and equally in need of protection. The perpetrator must be attended to and treated in order for the cycle to be interrupted. How can we go about treating a perpetrator who causes such damage to such vulnerable victims? How can we begin to see the perpetrator as a human being?

Although there are exceptions, due to the type of underlying pathology, most sexual abusers do not victimize because they need sexual stimulation.

Figure 1-1

THE BI-DIRECTIONAL CYCLE OF VICTIMIZATION

Forward Progression: Child Abuse

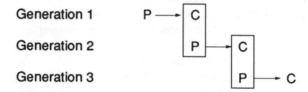

Generation 1	
Generation 2	
Generation 3	

Backward Progression: Elder Abuse

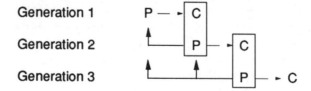

Generation 1	
Generation 2	
Generation 3	

As long as the pathology exists, the risk of continued victimization exists. Abusive behavior is the result of a dysfunctional perpetrator: the behavior is the *manifestation* of a pattern of either systematic or mental pathology that has been operating over time. The distinction between types of offenders will be elaborated in chapter 2, but for now we ask you to look at the perpetrator as a person whose own pain is being acted out in an inappropriate and destructive way.

The Victim in the Perpetrator

Because the sexual victimization of children is so abhorrent, the perpetrator is often perceived as some sort of monster. In our experience, this has not been the case. In our work with regressed-type perpetrators, sexual offenses have been the result of immature and inappropriate means of satisfying a need for love and affection rather than the result of malicious intent. The perpetrators we have worked with have been emotionally troubled and ill-equipped to handle stress in interpersonal relationships. Unfortunately, the majority had experienced abuse themselves (physical, emotional, or neglectful) during their childhood years, preventing them from feeling loved or cared for as adults and from becoming loving, care-giving parents. Many of them had been living law-abiding, normal lives until this exploitive behavior was triggered by some event or series of events. The seeds for the abuse are planted long before they germinate. When listening to perpetrators tell us the details of what they did to their children, we have to ask ourselves, "Where did they learn to do that?" "Where did they get the idea that was O.K. to do?" Almost without fail, what we get when we ask that question of the perpetrators is a long and pain-filled story of their own victimization—a story that usually sounds very similar to the abuse they have perpetrated on another. If we can begin to see that the perpetrator has also been a victim and has therefore had a dysfunctional learning history upon which was built a system of dysfunctional responses to anxiety and stress, we can begin to chase the monster away and see before us an injured human being who has, out of a very real pain and dysfunctional learning history, injured other human beings. If we can work on that unresolved pain, build a new repertoire of responses, heal the victim, heal the perpetrator, heal the broken relationship between victim and perpetrator, and heal the family, perhaps we can interrupt the cycle of intergenerational abuse. It is a tall order, but it is a place to start.

If counselors are to work with this population of clients, they must be willing to relate to them in a caring way. If the perpetrators' reasons for turning to children for satisfaction of their needs was that their adult relationships had become conflicted and emotionally unfulfilling, intimidating and disapproving intervenors would only exacerbate these problems. From the worker's perspective, it is imperative that the following provocative self-exploratory questions be asked:

- While my sympathy is with the abused child victim now, will my sympathies remain with the child when he or she in turn becomes an abuser?
- Am I capable of looking at an abuser and seeing the abused child he or she once was?
- Can I successfully intervene, conveying the toughness of the reality of the damage caused as well as tenderness in understanding how the abuser has come to this point?

We maintain that only when we can treat the perpetrator as a human being can we add therapeutic intervention to institutional punishment.

The Importance of Worker Self-Awareness

One of the ways in which a worker can begin to respond to those questions is to undertake an honest examination of personal experience. How is your experience with incest or abuse likely to influence your work with perpetrators? Unless you have worked through the issues around your own experiences, they will undoubtedly color, and probably interfere with, your work. Self-awareness is the key to planning and delivering client-focused intervention; it is difficult to keep the focus on the needs of the client and the client-system if your own needs interfere. We are all aware of the distortion the therapeutic relationship suffers when counter-transference becomes a party to the process. You may find that you need to work with a therapist to resolve your own issues. If so, we salute you for your courage and your professionalism! One of the ways we encourage workers to begin the self-awareness process in the workshops we conduct is to read aloud several blind case scenarios and then ask the attendees to take five minutes of quiet-time to write as quickly and as honestly as they can a letter of reaction to one of these perpetrators or to perpetrators of sexual offenses in general. Even though we are well aware that in any group of participants at our workshops there are several individuals who were themselves victims of sexual assault and who might never have felt safe enough to admit that experience to themselves or to anyone else, the letters they write are often overwhelming in their affective content. Here are two examples, the first written by a woman, the second written by a man:

> Dear Dick: You brought back for me all the pain, shame, and humiliation I suffered throughout my childhood and have fought so hard to keep from my awareness. As I write this letter, I am on fire with hatred and anger for all the rotten things you did to me and keep on doing to hurt me now, thirty

years later. I trusted you. You were my favorite uncle. How was I supposed to know that those "games" we played were wrong? When we first started playing it felt funny to me, but you told me, "Of course it's O.K., honey; Uncle Dick wouldn't do anything that wasn't right, would he? You don't need to ask Mommy if it's all right to play with your own Uncle Dick—after all, your Mom asked me to take care of you this weekend!" So I thought there must be something wrong with me. I still feel that way. There must be something wrong with me that I don't enjoy sex: everyone else in the world seems to love it! You did that to me, you bastard. You made me a prude. You ruined my marriage. You made me afraid of men. You made me hate sex. You made me hate my own son because he might grow up to be like you, like all men. But the worst thing you did was to make me doubt myself. I knew it was wrong, but you told me it wasn't. I knew I was doing something shameful, but you said it was O.K. I hate you. I hate you. I hate you, and I always will.

*　　　　*　　　　*

Dear Sarah: Why is it that women feel they have the right to use emotional blackmail, and get away with it? You see, you remind me of my *loving* grandmother who used to "enjoy so much" taking care of me. She would do the typical "female" things, like bake cookies, cakes, etc., and make me feel so special. I remember one manipulative act that she used frequently. If she asked me if I wanted to come to Grandma's and I said "no," she would say, "Well, I'll just have to give your surprise to Matt, if you don't want it." Oh, how that used to work. (You all know how to get us boys, don't you Sarah?) Well, let me tell you, this little boy grew up. The blinders are off. There won't be any fun baths with Grandma anymore, or any new "bathtub toys." You see, Grandma's favorite bathtub toy was me. I'm a homosexual, and proud of it, but I'll always wonder where I'd be now without my "loving Grandma." Thanks again Sarah, I now remember why I hate women.

These human service workers preparing themselves to work with perpetrators of sexual abuse bravely undertook the very serious and very painful work of honest self-awareness as a necessary step in their personal orientation to work of this kind. Because they were willing to take the risks inherent in that self-awareness process, they were able to begin the process of bringing their own biases to awareness and of purging themselves of the personal pain and unresolved issues that would otherwise most certainly have interfered with objective treatment. Here is an example of a letter one workshop attendee wrote to herself as a follow-up to the first exercise:

Dear _____: What a surprise it was for me to find out how deeply my feelings about perpetrators run! I had no idea I was so angry, or that that anger came from my love for Jack, who was so brutally abused as a child. I've watched how he has struggled to trust other people. I've listened in the dark to his cries when he has nightmares. I've choked down my own rage as I've listened to his stories of his childhood experiences with the people who abused him. And I marvel that he can sit at the same table with them year after year at Thanksgiving! If he can face his feelings, I can face mine. I wanted to help victims like Jack; I never dreamed I would have to try to help a perpetrator. Help them? I wanted to punish them! Now that I can see how that came from my anger over what happened to Jack, I see how important it is for me to work through those feelings—to at least be aware of them so I know when I'm responding from my own feelings and when I'm responding honestly to the people I'm working with. In order to do that, I resolve to: (a) try to get a handle on the perpetrator's side of the crime; (b) work hard in supervision to make sure I'm staying objective, and (c) seek therapy for myself if I find I am working on a self-responsive level with my clients.

Once we can honestly address our own ingrained response to sexual abuse in general, and to perpetrators of sexual abuse in particular, we can begin to clear the way for objective treatment. Awareness does not automatically eliminate bias. Once we have been directly or indirectly affected by the experience of sexual abuse, it is reasonable to expect that we will never forget that experience. But as direct or as vicarious victims, we can and we *must* embark on our own journey to forgiveness before we can be effective in helping someone else toward healing. Otherwise, we risk carrying our baggage into their treatment, and in the extreme, treating our experience rather than theirs.

As human service workers, we need to see abusers as human beings, replete with feelings and needs, hopes and aspirations—then perhaps we will be able to approach this deeply troubling human problem effectively through tough but tender intervention. We must, however, be realistic, we can't be bleeding hearts! Some perpetrators are more intractable than others; some are mentally impaired, some are encumbered with intractable personality disorders. While all perpetrators conform to the mental health model, not all perpetrators are untreatable. That's where the art and science of human service work comes into play: being informed and intuitive enough to know the difference, and being willing and able to advocate, design, carry out, and evaluate treatment. Perpetrators who are treated punitively rather than therapeutically may never have an opportunity to examine and understand the dynamics of their criminal behavior and may become prime candidates for perpetuated abuse. Traditionally, professional intervenors, by failing to treat known perpetrators of sexual abuse have in effect sent those untreated perpetrators back into the population to abuse again.

If we, who are trained to help people develop to their highest potential, cannot or will not treat the perpetrator in an attempt to intervene in the cycle of abuse, who will? It is important that we ask ourselves, "If this *perpetrator* were a member of my family, would I prefer jail with no treatment? Would I want my family committed to a future of social isolation and intrafamilial bitterness? If this *victim* were a member of my family, would I think that permanently cutting off contact with the abuser was best? Would I want to take the chance that some other family will suffer as mine has? Or am I willing to intervene in an attempt to change the scenario?

2
Perpetrator Assessment and Treatment

Where Do I Begin?

Although materials are available that take varied theoretical positions on the treatment of perpetrators, we do not intend to set forth a particular theory, but rather to extract from existing theory useful orientations for understanding assessment and treatment of perpetrators. While neither of us draws heavily on theory in working with perpetrators, some theoretical orientations have proven helpful. Especially for the worker new to dealing therapeutically with perpetrators, the pieces of theory we are about to present may help in developing a mindset from which to begin. We will begin by presenting a number of definitions of incest, and then we will proceed to a description of sexual offenses that constitute incest, which were developed by Dr. Suzanne Sgroi, then to looking at a typology of offenders, which was developed by Dr. A. Nicholas Groth. From there we will describe the W.A.R. Cycle developed by Ray Helfer. Together, these models help to clarify the distinctions between offenders and offenses and begin to establish a systems perspective on assessment, intervention, and treatment. The chapter will end with a discussion of recidivism.

At this point we would like to emphasize that, while this book presents material pertaining to both rapists and molesters, the bulk of our work has been with regressed molesters. We will therefore focus on the diagnosis and treatment of molesters. Many of the principles of treatment generalize to rapists as well, but there are also differences. Because molesters are more likely to select family members (or victims in family-like relationship), we will start by examining definitions of incest and incestuous acts.

Definitions of Incest

Generally, incest can be thought of as any form of sexual activity that occurs between a child and an adult family member, extended family member, or family-like member. Legal statute defines incest as specific sexual acts, usually involving intercourse, occurring between persons who would not be allowed to marry (family members). Another common definition says incest occurs when a family member in a more powerful role or position attempts to satisfy a sexual need with another less powerful family member. Generally, incest refers to the intrafamilial exploitation of a child under eighteen years of age who is not developmentally capable of understanding or resisting a sexual contact or who may be psychologically, physically, or socially dependent on the offender. Such sexual contact may range from exposure to penetration. We strongly agree with the preponderance of the literature that supports the stand that a child is *never* chargeable with the responsibility for consent in a sexual encounter, nor should we ever confuse cooperation and consent. In any relationship involving an adult and a child, the adult is *always* the responsible party, if for no other reason than because the adult is the larger and more powerful of the two.

Definitions of Incestuous Acts

Specifically, what kinds of sexual acts constitute incest? Suzanne Sgroi identifies a range of sexually abusive behaviors in her book, *Handbook of Clinical Intervention in Child Sexual Abuse*. We have seen examples of each type of sexually abusive behavior in our clinical experiences with victims and perpetrators.

The adult is nude in the presence of one or more non-spousal family members. A mother and her children who came to us for support in getting away from the husband/father complained that the father frequently sat in the living room totally nude. When the children protested the behavior, which prevented them from watching television, he would get up and stand in front of the television where they could not ignore him. If they attempted to leave the room, he would follow them and berate them for objecting to his "natural" state. Two of the children later disclosed ongoing sexual intercourse with the father.

The adult disrobes in the presence of one or more children. One adult child, still living in the household with young siblings, would regularly remove his clothing to bathe the younger children, explaining that he did not want to get his clothes wet.

The adult exposes his or her genitals to one or more children. One perpetrator described frequent experiences during which he would expose his penis to his young child and ask her to "make it grow" by "petting it."

The adult is unnecessarily present while the child is nude or is eliminating. One victim described how uncomfortable she still is changing clothes in a room or bathroom without a lockable door. She remembers her father persisting in being present whenever she used the bathroom. He insisted it was a father's duty to be sure she was developing properly and was regular in her elimination functions.

The adult kisses the child in a way that is uncomfortable for the child. One male victim-survivor remembers being ill at ease with the way his adult aunt would hold him close in sustained kisses when no one else was around.

The adult fondles the child and/or has the child fondle the adult. One perpetrator, while babysitting with his girlfriend's child, would complain of a headache and go to the bedroom to lay down. When the child would come to ask if he was feeling better, he would ask the child to rub his head, then his chest, then his genitals. As the child would rub him, he would reciprocally rub the child "so the child could see how good it felt."

The adult masturbates himself, masturbates the child, watches the child masturbate himself or herself, or engages in mutual masturbation. A perpetrator told the group how he "got off" knowing that a neighbor's son was watching at a distance through the screen door as he masturbated. After that he would invite the child to come into the house to watch him as "a lesson in manhood." He taught the child to masturbate, watching to be sure the boy did it right. Eventually, the perpetrator and the ten-year-old masturbated each other in a contest to see which of them could ejaculate first.

The adult performs fellatio on the child or encourages the child to perform fellatio on the adult. A female victim-survivor recalled how her father invited her into his bed to cuddle her when her mother worked nights. She remembers falling asleep, then awakening to find her father forcing his penis into her mouth. A young male victim-survivor remembers awakening in the night to find his grandfather sucking on his penis.

The adult performs cunnilingus on the child or encourages the child to perform cunnilingus on the adult. When a mother suddenly came into the bathroom during bath time and found her husband appearing to blow into the child's vagina, the child playfully explained, "We're playing whales! Daddy is making sure my blow hole isn't blocked again." In another case, little Janet told the investigator that the (female) babysitter said girls tasted sweet inside and that if Janet would taste her, the baby-sitter would taste Janet.

The adult places a finger or an object into the child's anus or rectum. Chuckie's aunt would spank him with her hand, then put her finger into his rectum "to be sure she had spanked all the shit out."

An adult male penetrates the anus or rectum of the child with his penis. Phillip wouldn't let the hospital do a rectal exam, and tearfully described to his doctor how his abuser put his penis into Phillip's rectum, pushed it in until Phillip started to cry, then berated Phillip for crying "like a wimpy little kid."

The adult puts a finger or an object into the vagina of a child. At first, Karen told us, her uncle would just want to put a finger in her vagina; he didn't start using a bottle until she was ten. On returning from her father's house after a weekend visit, four-year-old Angela was observed probing her vagina with crayons. When asked what she was doing, Angela said, "Daddy does it."

The adult male penetrates the vagina of a child with his penis. Marsha's mother became suspicious when eight-year-old Marsha requested an appointment with the doctor. As it turned out, Marsha had a sexually transmitted disease.

An adult male rubs his penis against a child's genitals, rectum, thigh, or buttocks. Richard told his counselor that he saw nothing wrong with making his child squirm around on his lap until he became erect because he never penetrated her.

According to Sgroi, there is usually a progression from less intimate sexual acts to body contact to some form of penetration. Our experience confirms the existence of a progression of contact among regressed and fixated molesters. Such a progression is unlikely with rapists. Rapists generally are not concerned with gaining the confidence of their victims or with making sure the victim is comfortable with the sexual contact so it can proceed in secret. Rapists usually act to overpower the victim and satisfy some need of their own. The progression of sexual contact, designed to gradually involve the victim and gain his or her trust and confidence, is one way to distinguish a molester from a rapist. Molestation tends to be more gradually seductive in nature; rape tends to be more aggressive with little or no thought to the welfare of the victim. To further clarify similarities and differences, we share with you A. Nicholas Groth's typology of offenders, which we find most useful in assessment and treatment planning.

Groth's Typology of Pedophilic Offenders

Extrapolating from two of his books, *Sexual Assault of Children and Adolescents* and *Men Who Rape: The Psychology of the Offender* (coauthored with H. Jean Birnbaum), A. Nicholas Groth classifies sexual offenses into two main categories: rape and molestation. Groth estimates that 15 to 20 percent of sexual offenses against children are rape and 80 to 85 percent are molestation. Both the M.O. and the psychopathology of the rapist vary significantly from that of the molester; thus, therapeutic issues differ for rapists and molesters. While rape is usually an expression of rage, power needs, and sadistic pleasure, by comparison, molestation is a seductive act in which the offender seeks mutual enjoyment, acceptance, and affection. Molesters tend to take the time to set up the victim with a progression of behavior beginning with non-genital acts and progressing to genital acts—they seem to want a compliant victim. The rapist spontaneously forces himself on his victim with no thought for whether the victim is comfortable in participating. Both rape and molestation are abusive; the differences are in the manner in which the abuse is manifested, the motivation of the abuser, and the magnitude of force or violence used.

Groth draws clear differentiations between three types of rape/rapists: anger, power, sadistic, and between two types of molestation/molesters: regressed and fixated, referring to the course of development of the offenders' social and sexual orientations. In our experience, it is of primary importance to be able to assess whether the offender is of the regressed type or of the fixated type. Although we always work with the perpetrators individually before any therapeutic contact is made with the family, we need to make a determination as to whether the offender's sociosexual development was *fixated* (stopped or arrested) during their childhood, adolescence, or early adult years, or whether their primary sociosexual interest had been with age-mates until their response to an identifiable stressor caused them to *regress* to an earlier stage of development where functioning in the world was manageable and less anxiety-laden. Our experience is consistent with Groth's: the majority of perpetrators we see are of the regressed type.

The term *regressed offender* refers to an emotional regression. An outgrowth of the Freudian perspective, regression occurs when an individual who has developed normally to a given point (in this case, has experienced normal emotional development) reverts to an earlier point of development that was in some way more comfortable or more secure than the age-appropriate developmental level. This type of offender tends to be deeply affected by *inter*personal dynamics, especially family dynamics. For this type of offender, family dynamics play an important role in determining the situational precursors to the offense and play an important role in the healing process of the perpetrator and the family system. The regressed offender is usually active with a limited number of victims, usually family members or family-like in their relationship to the perpetrator.

The *fixated offender,* by contrast, experiences an interruption in emotional development, which causes sociosexual development to stop at a given point and remain fixed. The fixated offender focuses on *intra*personal dynamics and tends to seek non-family victims. Usually the fixated offender is active with a larger number of victims than the regressed offender.

In his chapter, "The Incest Offender" in *Handbook of Clinical Intervention in Child Sexual Abuse* by Suzanne Sgroi, Groth distinguishes the regressed and fixated pedophilic offenders from one another by the following characteristics:

1. **The *primary sexual* orientation of the regressed offender is to age-mates.** The adult offender is normally attracted to age-mates when in an unstressed condition. Regressed offenders usually are or have been married, and both parties to the marriage have, at some point, been satisfied with that marital relationship. Most regressed offenders went through all the ordinary stages of social and heterosexual development that normal young people go through. Most have never experienced abnormal homosexual tendencies, nor have they been attracted to partners outside the normal age-mate parameters. If they had a clear choice, they would choose to relate sexually to an age-mate.

   The *primary* sexual orientation of the fixated offender is to children. This type of offender prefers to relate sexually to a child. Given a choice between an age-mate sexual partner and a child sexual partner, the fixated offender will be attracted to the child. Most fixated offenders have never had satisfying relationships with age-mates and often have never been attracted strongly enough to an age-mate to have developed a formalized relationship.

2. **Pedophilic interests of the regressed offender emerge in *adulthood*.** When assessing the developmental history of the perpetrator, the regressed offender's pattern of relationships will show no sexual attraction to younger partners before adulthood. The sexual interest in children develops only after the regressed offender has developed satisfying relationships with age-mates in adulthood.

   Pedophilic interests of the fixated offender emerge in *adolescence*. Many fixated offenders report that they didn't *become* interested in children sexually, they *discovered* their sexual orientation, usually as they watched their adolescent peers developing an interest in the opposite sex, an interest they did not share. For these fixated offenders, any relationships with age-mates in adulthood were motivated by a desire to "cover" for their orientation to children or to attempt to prove to themselves or others that their development was normal in comparison with the sexual orientation of their peers.

3. **For the regressed offender, a** *precipitating stressor* **is usually evident or identifiable.** Common precipitating events for regressed offenders are experiences such as death of a significant other, job loss, physical disability, marital disintegration, or some other event or combination of events that is likely to result in significant loss of self-esteem, control, or power for the perpetrator. Unresolved grief or loss is a common precursor to abuse in the families we have worked with.

   For the fixated offender, there is *no precipitating stressor.* The fixated offender does not become sexually attentive to children as a result of a stressor, but rather is showing a specific sexual orientation. The fixated offender is not reacting to subjective distress, but is merely expressing sexual needs with a person perceived to be a cooperative peer.

4. **For the regressed offender, sexually abusive acts may be** *episodic.* The regressed offender may be sexually active with the victim only when experiencing periods of extreme stress or low self-esteem. When the environmental stressors are at an ebb, the regressed offender may not approach a child at all, but rather may find relationships with age-mates satisfactory.

   In contrast, the fixated offender exhibits *persistent* pedophilic interest. The fixated offender's sexual attraction to children is compulsive and chronic. While the regressed offender turns to children in times of extreme stress, the fixated offender consistently prefers children.

5. **For the regressed offender, the initial sexual offense may be** *impulsive.* The regressed offender may not plan a sexual encounter with a child. Sexual activity often happens spontaneously in a time of extreme stress when the perpetrator is experiencing feelings of shame, inadequacy, and low self-esteem. For example, a father may babysit for his children on numerous occasions without any intention of abusing the child. Yet, on one particular night, when he is at an all-time low, he impulsively invites the child into his bed to comfort him. Afterward he is shocked and dismayed at his own behavior.

   For the fixated offender, the sexual offense is *preplanned.* The fixated offender is inclined to set up the victim, to slowly condition the victim over time in order to prepare the victim for the sexual act. The fixated offender may begin by checking out how willing a participant a given child might be, then start the conditioning process by telling the child stories, sharing pornographic materials, coaxing the child into pornographic-like acts with treats or subtle threats, engaging the child in pornographic acts, and then progress to engaging the child in sexual activity. By contrast to the example given for the impulsive regressed offender, the fixated offender would spend considerable time and effort preparing the child until the child seemed old enough and engaged enough to begin sexual activity without endangering the perpetrator.

6. **The regressed offender substitutes the child for a peer.** The regressed offender ends a conflicted relationship with a peer and substitutes a less conflicted relationship with a child. In the perception of the perpetrator, the child victim attains pseudo-adult status. Because of a precipitating stressor, the adult regresses to the emotional level of a child and the child is elevated by the perpetrator to a stage similar to that of the perpetrator. The perpetrator misperceives the child as a consenting adult. In a case in which the perpetrator is the parent of the victim, the parent usually abandons the parental role in favor of a peer relationship with the "adultified" child.

   The fixated offender identifies with the child victim. Rather than elevating the child to a perceived adult level, the adult becomes a pseudochild. Developmentally, the adult becomes childlike.

   It is interesting that both the regressed and the fixated offender achieve a perceived peer relationship with the victim: one by misperceiving the child as an adult, the other by misperceiving himself or herself as a child.

7. **The regressed offender's primary targets are opposite-sex victims.**
   The fixated offender's primary targets are same-sex victims.

8. **For the regressed offender, sexual contact with a child occurs concurrent with sexual contact with age-mates.** Many regressed offenders are either married or living in a committed relationship with an age-mate. It may, in fact, be that instability in this primary relationship is the precipitating stressor that contributes to or causes the onset of sexual abuse. What we usually see is that the primary relationship continues somewhat intact until the abuse is disclosed, and surprisingly enough, it is often resumed once the disclosure occurs and the initial crisis abates. Many of the incarcerated perpetrators we have worked with leave prison to resume their marriages, all too often without sufficiently working through the aftermath of the abuse and the adjudication.

   For the fixated offender, there is little or no sexual contact with age-mates. A majority of fixated offenders are single or living in a "marriage of convenience" and have limited, if any, sexual contact with age-mates as a matter of preference.

9. **The regressed offender tends to focus on his or her own sexual arousal and satisfaction.**
   The fixated offender tends to seek sexual arousal on the part of the child victim.

10. **For the regressed offender, the offense is more likely to be *alcohol-related* than for the fixated offender.** The regressed offender, as we have already mentioned, is likely to be reacting sexually to a stressor. It is often the case that the regressed offender uses alcohol to numb the anxiety. The alcohol tends to anesthetize inhibitions against such social taboos as incest and child abuse, thereby increasing the likelihood of an impulsive act on what are otherwise inhibited primary impulses.

    For the fixated offender, there is usually *no alcohol or drug use.*

11. **The regressed offender is likely to lead a fairly traditional lifestyle but have poorly developed peer relationships.** Often, the regressed offender adheres to traditional values and considers those values to be very important. Yet, because of an inability to maintain satisfactory peer relationships (due, perhaps to an inability to cope appropriately with stress in interpersonal relationships), the regressed offender looks to children with whom to have a less-risk relationship. Often, these are men who have had devastating relationships with adult women during their lifetimes, leaving them easily hurt, humiliated, or rebuffed by female agemates. They may appear strong in the relationship, but feel powerless and childlike in comparison with the woman. While they maintain defendable values in other areas of their lives, their values concerning mates or sexual partners are easily manipulated or abandoned in an effort to achieve closeness and intimacy.

    The fixated offender exhibits *chronic immaturity*. This offender's history shows a consistent pattern of poor sociosexual relationships with peers. This makes sense when we consider that the fixated offender's emotional development was arrested at some point short of maturity. Because of the developmental deficit, Groth's experience is that the fixated offender is more difficult to treat than the regressed offender. Our experience agrees with Groth's. The fixated offender is an appropriate candidate for developmental therapy, which is time consuming, requires specialized training, and is difficult to do in a prison setting or under extreme stress.

12. **The regressed offender abuses as a response to *overwhelming life stress*.** The offender displays the ability to cope adequately most of the time, but when the stressor or combination of stressors is great, reverts to inferior coping mechanisms and focuses on seeking comfort and satisfaction while disregarding or even failing to consider the needs of the victim.

    The fixated offender abuses in response to *developmental life issues*. Rather than reacting to a specific identifiable stressor, the fixated offender develops deviant sexual behavior as a maladaptive response to seemingly unresolvable pervasive issues surrounding his or her own development.

Pedophile Offenders Versus Hebephile Offenders

Groth makes a distinction between a pedophile offender and a hebephile offender. Pedophiles are people who, as sexual maturation begins, discover that they are primarily or exclusively attracted to pre-adolescent children. In contrast, hebephiles find themselves sexually attracted to young teenagers or adolescents. The distinction is made according to the age group of the child whom the perpetrator victimizes. In terms of treatment, such a distinction is helpful in determining at what point of emotional development the perpetrator is fixated or has regressed. Once that stage of development has been identified, the clinician can begin to pinpoint the developmental issues from which to begin planning treatment.

Using Groth's Differentiations for Treatment Planning

There are five points to consider in making differentiations between types of offenders and offenses in devising a treatment plan. According to Groth, treatment planning proceeds based on criteria similar to these. (For a more detailed discussion of criteria, see Groth's article, "Guidelines for the Assessment and Management of the Offender," in Burgess, Groth, Holmstrom, and Sgroi.)

The Nature of the Crime

Was the offense planned? Was it intentional? Was the victim set up? Was the offensive behavior a response to an interpersonal problem? Can the behavior be treated effectively to assure that it will not reoccur? If we can establish that the perpetrator's primary and persistent sexual attraction is to same-sex children, that the child was set up with malicious intent, manipulated into position, and then trapped in some manner into cooperation and secrecy, the offender is probably of the fixated type. If that is the case, there are options to be considered: (1) if you are not adequately trained or if you are uncomfortable working with fixated offenders, you can and *should* refer for developmental or specialized treatment; (2) you may choose to press for incarceration; or (3) you may choose to press for treatment in a secure facility other than a prison or jail.

If, on the other hand, you find the perpetrator has a history of satisfying sexual relationships with opposite sex age-mates, demonstrated no malicious intent, has lead a fairly traditional lifestyle, and was acting maladaptively in response to an identifiable stressor or series of stressors, the options may be different: (1) if you are not adequately trained or if you are uncomfortable working with regressed molesters, you can and *should* refer to an appropriate service provider; (2) you may press for incarceration; (3) you may press for treatment in a non-secure facility; (4) you may press for community-based treatment and probation; or (5) if you are an experienced worker and have reason to have confidence in your client's commitment to treatment and behavior change, you may work with the perpetrator and family in independent practice, assuming the court is agreeable. We recommend that if you choose to work in independent practice, you impose strong external controls on the therapeutic relationship to ensure continued progress. Such controls might be connection and cooperation with probation or court officers, social workers, and CPS workers. A written contract is helpful in maintaining an understanding that if there is any violation of the terms of the legal agreement, you will take immediate action to intervene *and* that the perpetrator agrees to submit to a more restrictive means of treatment.

It is imperative that in determining the conditions of your treatment plan, *first consideration be given to the physical and emotional safety and well-being of the victim or victims*. When we have chosen to work with perpetrators in private practice, we are aware, and the court makes it clear, that we are taking on a serious responsibility. That, too, needs to be taken into consideration: are you willing to take on the responsibility for the safety of the family and the community by working with this client in private practice?

The Risk of Continued Offense

Statistically, fixated offenders are more likely to abuse again than regressed offenders. The typing of offender and offense may one day become a critical factor in the adjudication and sentencing process, and we assert that it should. We will explore this issue in more detail in chapter 4. The risk of continued offense should be a critical factor in determining how secure or restrictive the treatment environment needs to be. As a professional, you may choose to advocate for treatment in more secure environments for rapists and fixated molesters and less secure environments for regressed molesters. As of this writing, the legal system has not yet come to a level of sophistication by which sexual abuse cases are adjudicated differentially according to these distinctions. When writing court reports or progress summaries to lawyers, law guardians, or other involved judicial officers, seize the opportunity to do some educating. Use these distinctions as diagnostic tools justifying differential sentencing and treatment implications. Use your knowledge and position as treatment provider and advocate to influence the system toward precision in diagnosis and treatment. Remember that our purpose is to intervene in and prevent ongoing abuse and thereby protect victims and potential victims. Therefore, *first consideration must be given to the physical and emotional safety and well-being of the victim, victims, or potential victims*.

The Treatment of Choice

The treatment of choice for the regressed offender is likely to involve inter-personal and intrafamilial issues such as exploration of personal stressors, exploration of the perpetrator's learning history around coping mechanisms for stress, work around self-esteem, peer relationships, relationships with the opposite sex, parenting, boundary issues, substance abuse, taking responsi-bility for offensive behavior, and restitution.

The treatment of choice for the fixated offender is more likely to be de-velopmental in nature. Treatment will likely involve issues such as develop-ment of sexual orientation, sexual identity issues, pedophilic preoccupation, manipulative behaviors, social development and arrest, emotional develop-ment and arrest, and coping and adaptation methods as well as the interper-sonal and intrafamilial issues listed for the regressed offender.

The Prognosis for Recovery or Rehabilitation

Regardless of typology, the prognosis is for lifetime management. The of-fenders are always in danger of reoffending and will need to learn to monitor and control their behavior *for the rest of their lives.* We need to consider the risk to the community and to past and potential victims when considering a treatment plan. What kinds of services will the perpetrator need lifelong? How can we best ensure those service connections will be made? The need for lifetime management became clear to us when, nearing termination from group, an incarcerated offender made a casual remark indicating that he had regressed in his treatment. Here is a clinical example:

> One of us was working with a formerly incarcerated perpetrator once he had returned to his family and community. The family had experienced a substantial amount of healing, to the point that we were advocating to ob-tain permission from the court for the youngest daughter, now a young adult, to return to the home of her parents (at her request and the parents' joyful agreement). When the perpetrator (who had now been in the com-munity nearly six months) presented his case for immediate reunion, despite the mother's and daughter's hesitation to reunite the family abruptly, his statements began with phrases like, "I've decided," "I want," "I think." In the face of this new stressor (the possibility that he might be unable to have what he wanted), he was reverting to his former controlling style of behavior despite the contrary wishes of the victims. When he was confronted with the tough reality of his regression and tender understanding of his fears that his daughter might not be permitted to return to his home, he dissolved into tears. The session ended by bringing the wife and daughter into the room so the perpetrator could apologize to them, confess his fears, and ask their forgiveness for his behavior.

The client's prognosis for and degree of recovery or rehabilitation should directly influence your planning or recommendations for discharge and follow-up treatment. We would like to see some legal teeth put into these recommendations. At present, once an offender has served a prison term or been discharged by the court, there is no means of maintaining contact or of mandating any further conditions. We would like to see judicial reform at both ends of the continuum: (1) a stop to plea bargaining to a comparable but non-sex-crime-related offense; (2) a mandate to treatment; and (3) a follow-up component consisting of extended parole contact and mandated connection with community-based treatment and lifetime monitoring. Here too there is opportunity for professional advocacy for judicial reform. We encourage you to use whatever contact you have with the courts or the legal system to educate and advocate.

Reintegration of the Perpetrator

The perpetrator is going to have to learn to live among people in a new and more adaptive way. It does not make sense to us to lock up a regressed offender forever. What does make sense is to teach the perpetrator how to live without offending and that he or she alone is responsible for the offense and bears a major portion of the responsibility for enabling the victim's healing. If you find that your client is of the fixated type, you will need to exercise extreme caution in recommending discharge from treatment into the community without careful monitoring and mandatory service connection.

At present, New York State rigorously restricts a sex-offender parolee's access to children. Before release on parole, the perpetrator must provide evidence that neither his or her living situation (choice of home or apartment, proximity to schools or playgrounds, members of the household) nor work situation (place of employment, type of employment, nature of the work) allow *any* access to children. If there is a child household member, if the house or apartment is close to a school, playground, or other place where children are likely to be; if the offender's work involves proximity to children (such as apartment maintenance, school staff, playground supervision or maintenance, teaching, daycare, or youthwork,) parole will be denied until evidence is provided that the offender has *no* access to children. For fixated offenders, these restrictions are good prevention—they at least make it more difficult for a chronic offender to make connections with children. For treated regressed molesters they seem overly restrictive. Regressed molesters are more likely to target family or family-like members as victims, thereby posing little threat to extra-familial children. We concur that newly treated perpetrators are not ready to be in close contact with child family members. Without extensive preparation, we would not risk additional trauma to the victim by reuniting the perpetrator with the family or family-like household until more than adequate preparation had been made and all parties (especially the victim and non-victimized children) express readiness.

As it happens, most of the perpetrators we have worked with do return to their marital partners. In many cases, the children have grown up and moved away while the offender has been in prison—usually putting great geographic obstacles between them. In some cases, the children have been placed in foster care or have been released for adoption. In other cases, the crime occurred with a child of a lover or common-law partner. Sometimes the spouse divorces the perpetrator, or the lover or common-law partner leaves the relationship—and sometimes leaves the community or region. We believe the perpetrator's access to children remaining in the household with which he intends to unite or reunite should be controlled. Preparation needs to be made, the interests of the victim need to be paramount in making a reunite or separate decision, there needs to be demonstrated behavior change, marital work needs to be done to resolve the dysfunctions that contributed to the initial offense, family work needs to be done, victim and perpetrator work needs to be done, forgiveness work needs to be done, trust needs to be built back up. Supervision and monitoring needs to be arranged to the satisfaction of the family and the professional intervenors. Service connection and monitoring for the perpetrator needs to be in place and working effectively. We are talking about a huge investment in professional time and energy—and we all know that means a huge financial investment as well. All these factors need to be considered when we evaluate the client's prognosis for social and familial adjustment. On the judicial level, we need to work toward funding these services. As expensive as they are when projected over a lifetime, the cost of differential diagnosis, sentencing, and treatment, combined with community-based service connection, community-based follow-up treatment, and lifelong monitoring, is small when compared with the cost of excessive incarceration.

Groth's typology should give you some basis for assessing the perpetrator so that you can begin to conceptualize an appropriate treatment plan. We hope you also begin to see how pervasive the pathology can be and how important it is that you understand the need to refer appropriately. Not all of us are equipped with both the skills and the stamina to treat perpetrators. Some seem to be intractable. One of the things that Groth's typology enables us to do is a sort of triage assessment: which offenders can we help and which can we not help? Treat those you can, take them as far as you are able to take them, know when you are in over your head, then refer to responsible service providers who can continue the work of lifelong management and monitoring.

Perhaps an example of a regressed offender and an example of a fixated offender will be useful at this point. As the cases are presented, use the diagnostic skills you have acquired to conceptualize a diagnosis and formulate treatment recommendations of each case.

Steve had been married to Phyllis for ten years and had two stepdaughters, twelve-year-old Stephanie and thirteen-year-old Dawn. He regarded the children as his own and had a trusting and close emotional relationship with them. When he lost his job due to a layoff, he lost his position as breadwinner and also his self-esteem. To compensate, he assumed full control over the house and everyone in it, running the household like a military installation. Phyllis was earning enough money at her job that she could support the family until he found work, but things were tight. Phyllis was in ill health and in need of a hysterectomy and was unable to engage in sexual activity with Steve. In order to economize during the cold months, Phyllis and Steve decided they would move their bed into the living room and close off the large bedroom, saving them a considerable amount of money on heating bills. In fact, they lowered the temperature in the entire house. While Phyllis worked, Steve watched television in bed. The girls often climbed in beside him, fully dressed, to watch television in warmth and comfort. One afternoon, Stephanie went to visit a friend, leaving Dawn and Steve alone. Steve had been drinking and was unusually relaxed. He reached over to touch Dawn and placed his hand on her breast. She protested mildly and Steve withdrew his hand. After that Dawn noticed that Steve favored her with privileges she had not been allowed previously, but only as long as she focused her attention on him. When she indicated an interest in an age-mate, he became jealous and grounded her. (It appeared, in talking to Steve, that he was attracted to Dawn as if he were courting her. With Phyllis so sick, money so tight, and Steve's self-esteem at such a low point, the momentary closeness with Dawn was misinterpreted by Steve as peer intimacy.) Upset by what was occurring, Dawn told Phyllis what had happened. When Phyllis confronted Steve, he said he didn't remember touching Dawn; he had been drinking. Phyllis accepted his excuse, told him never to touch Dawn again, and never mentioned the incident to Dawn again. After three or four repetitions of similar episodes, Dawn finally told the school nurse what had happened to her. When Steve was approached by a police officer and a child protection worker, he immediately confessed and asked for help.

*   *   *

Meanwhile, but in a different setting, I was working with a client I shall call Bob. Bob was an incarcerated offender who told his story to the group of perpetrators we facilitated. He was a middle class man who worked as a groundskeeper for a large university. At the age of seventeen, Bob realized that he was different from other guys his age: while the others were interested in girls, he found himself attracted to age-mate men. He was aware that his sexual interest was unusual, so he began to cover his interest in men with a pseudo-interest in women. Even though he found heterosexual relationships unsatisfying, he conceded to the social pressure to marry; a self-described "marriage of convenience" that continued for twenty-two years, during which he fathered four children. He chose to maintain a separate apartment close to campus and would invite groups of young boys from the community to use his apartment to "party." There they would congregate to play cards, listen to music, and "rap," restricted only to cleaning up after themselves. Gradually, the card games progressed to strip poker, and the rapping progressed to lewd sexual acts, often involving the taking of pornographic photographs. Eventually, a neighbor reported the suspicious behavior, the apartment was searched, and the photographs were found. Bob insisted he had no knowledge of what was going on; he was an innocent bystander—he had never meant for it to happen and was "sucked into" the activity only after it had been going on for a long time. When questioned about his participation, he said, "I wanted it to end, but didn't know how to stop it." The investigation revealed that the sex parties had been going on for four or five years.

A Conceptual Framework: The W.A.R. Cycle

Ray Helfer introduced the W.A.R. Cycle in his work, *The Diagnostic Process and Treatment Programs,* in 1977. Since that time, it has become one of the classic conceptual tools used for gaining understanding of and insight into the family dynamics that foster physical, emotional, and sexual abuse and neglect. (See figure 2–1.)

W.A.R. stands for the World of Abnormal Rearing. Helfer traces a pattern wherein individuals reared in the W.A.R. cycle often seek self-fulfillment through extra-familial relationships, escaping from their abusive family of origin through untimely marriage or pregnancy in an attempt to fill the unsatisfied needs of childhood. The child-turned-parent transfers to the next-generation child unrealistic expectations for meeting the needs of the parent. In an effort to satisfy the parent's need to be taken care of, the child reverses roles with the parent. The child is unable to satisfy the parent's expectations, and the parents become frustrated and abuse the child as punishment, which is a learned response from the parent's childhood experience. As a result, the child develops a lack of trust in people, isolates himself or herself for protection against shame, is robbed of normal child development in deference to parenting the parent, and develops a self-concept of "bad kid," "flawed," or "different." Into adulthood, the abused or neglected child has a hard time making friends due to the burden of internalized shame, and low self-esteem, and arrested development. In search of a way out, the child makes one or more untimely choices of mates in attempts to escape the oppressive expectations and abuses of the parent and to satisfy his or her own unmet needs. The female child is likely to impulsively conceive a child, anticipating that in the infant she will finally have a warm, cuddly little one to lavish her love

Figure 2-1

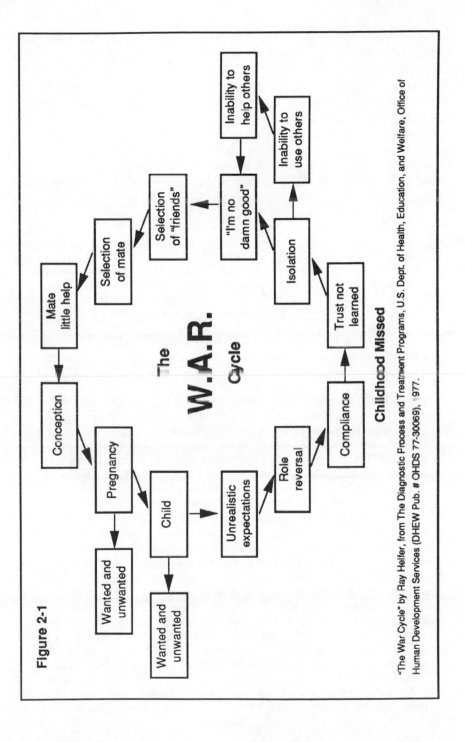

The
W.A.R.
Cycle

Conception → Pregnancy

Mate little help ← Conception

Selection of mate ← Mate little help

Selection of "friends" ← Selection of mate

Inability to help others

Inability to use others

"I'm no damn good"

Isolation

Trust not learned

Pregnancy → Wanted and unwanted

Pregnancy → Child

Child → Wanted and unwanted

Child → Unrealistic expectations

Unrealistic expectations → Role reversal

Role reversal → Compliance

Compliance → Trust not learned

Childhood Missed

"The War Cycle" by Ray Helfer, from The Diagnostic Process and Treatment Programs, U.S. Dept. of Health, Education, and Welfare, Office of Human Development Services (DHEW Pub. # OHDS 77-30069), 1977.

upon, to "raise better than her parents raised her," who will love her uncon-
ditionally in return. But the unrelenting dependency of an infant, the temper
tantrums of childhood, and the overwhelming responsibilities of parenthood
frustrate that expectation of unconditional love. The parent, unable to deal
appropriately with her own pain, places unrealistic expectations on the child,
setting the whole cycle into repetition. Unless intervention occurs, this cycle
is likely to continue repeating from generation to generation. In the case of
sexual abuse, it follows logically that what one learns from one's own experience, one is likely to repeat with one's own children, especially in times of
stress. So the child victim becomes the adult perpetrator, responding to stress
and pain in the same dysfunctional way his or her parents did.

To better illustrate the W.A.R. Cycle, let's look at a case:

Duane, a sixteen-year-old boy, first came to see me after he fondled his three-
year-old brother. Duane was visibly upset, and said he needed help because
of what he had done. With total lack of affect, he related his story of abuse
(in nondescript details) and told me that he had seen a counselor in another
state for about six weeks, right after the disclosure of the abuse. He stated
that he thought he "had it together" then, but now he wasn't so sure; he was
frightened by his own feelings and behavior. For fourteen weeks, Duane and
I talked about his own abuse at the hand of his stepfather, which started
when he was three (note the age pattern) and continued until he disclosed it
at fourteen. Duane's stepfather had abused drugs and alcohol, becoming
physically abusive, and then "making it up to Duane" through sexual abuse.
Eventually the stepfather began allowing friends to "use" Duane, and the
threats became more and more violent if the "secret" was ever revealed. Since
Duane's Mom worked the 11:00 A.M. to 7:00 P.M. shift, Duane never knew
when his Dad would "throw a party." Eventually, the abusive situation became so severe that Duane ended up in the hospital, where he finally felt
safe enough to disclose. Throughout the disclosure process, Duane was unable to express any emotion. When asked how he felt, he would say "I don't
know." This continued for fourteen weeks until finally, in the middle of a
Monopoly game (we played games as part of therapy because Duane had
never had any constructive playful experience and said he didn't really have
any close friends and was afraid to make friends because he "didn't even
know how to play a game"), he started to choke and sobbed uncontrollably:
the emotional dam had finally broken. As therapy progressed it became evident that Duane was caught up in the W.A.R. cycle. He finally told me he
was intimately involved with a fourteen-year-old girl; neither was using protection against conception because they "wanted a baby." He had been caring for his two younger brothers for years and wanted a family of his own.
Looking back at family history, Duane had started to abuse his brother as
he had been abused. His mother's history revealed that she conceived Duane
out of wedlock when she was fifteen years old. She had come from a physically and emotionally abusive home and her father was alcoholic. When

Duane was born, she developed some very unrealistic goals for herself, and eventually for Duane as well. She looked to Duane to "father" the two younger boys and to give her the unconditional love that she had been seeking for so long. Now Duane was looking for a way out—for someone who could love him for who he was and for someone to call his own. Duane's mother, unable to get her needs met, charged her son with responsibility for meeting them without consideration for his needs. In turn, Duane, physically and emotionally damaged, and with unmet needs of his own, dragged his emotional baggage into an untimely union, charging his yet unborn child with the task of meeting his overwhelming needs.

And so it goes; the W.A.R. Cycle repeats itself, sometimes for generations.

Recidivism: Another Vicious Cycle

The social consensus that perpetrators of sexual abuse should be locked up and the key thrown away has not developed in a vacuum. Historically, the likelihood of recidivism (repeated crimes) for a perpetrator of sexual abuse has been extremely high, so society's curative response to those convicted of incestuous crimes has been lengthy incarceration: "punish them and they will stop doing it." It is a common assumption that in keeping with the inherent "family secret" associated with sex crimes, these perpetrators actively avoid counseling, even while incarcerated. In truth, rehabilitation is not offered or available in most state prison facilities. Our experience has been that where such a program exists, the demand exists. Lorne Jepson, the corrections counselor who cofacilitated our groups (and is still facilitating groups for incarcerated rapists and molesters) was asked by inmates on a regular basis when they could get into one of our groups. Needless to say, the problem that caused them to abuse had never before been dealt with. Even if perpetrators are determined never to hurt a child again, they have more than likely learned their deeply ingrained abusive response during childhood or lacked the functional coping skills necessary to deal with stressful situations. Under these circumstances, the untreated offender is highly likely to repeat the patterned and dysfunctional response to stress—to abuse again. We would like to think that was the inmates' primary motivation. In some cases, it was. In other cases the inmates were eager to participate in voluntary programming to make their records look good before appearing before a parole board. We let the pressures inherent in the system funnel inmates into the program for screening. We would then screen them for group suitability, sincerity of intent, amenability to treatment, and commitment to therapy. We found the process to be an effective mechanism for recruiting suitable group members. The system doesn't always work against us!

Because of the lack of professional training and the stigma associated with this type of crime, professionals often feel ill-equipped to work with perpetrators and actively seek to avoid the perpetrator population. In our experience, there are men who can resume a normal life and appropriate sexual relationships after therapeutic intervention. (Once again, we are not "bleeding hearts" and are not naïve enough to think that all perpetrators of sexual abuse can be rehabilitated and trusted around children again. But to reiterate, these people, no matter what their typology, once out of prison, are a danger to every child *unless we intervene therapeutically.* Remember, our primary purpose is to protect and promote the healing of the abused child and to help prevent further abuse. It is self-evident then that we cannot "keep our hands clean" by working only with victims while avoiding comprehensive intervention with the perpetrator. If we choose to avoid working with perpetrators, our children are at risk.

The models we have provided to this point highlight the complexity of the problem of perpetration of sexual and incestuous acts. Understanding that complexity, perhaps you can identify with our frustration over the isolated and simplistic means of treatment that exist. For some individuals, incarceration is one form of therapy. In our estimation, however, incarceration isn't nearly enough. When incarceration is appropriate, it needs to be supplemented with incest-specific treatment, and the perpetrator needs to be followed into the community with community-based, family-oriented, comprehensive, lifelong treatment. Where incarceration is not indicated, we see a need for a comprehensive program of individual and family incest-specific treatment, combined with an ongoing community-based support program enabling the perpetrator to self-monitor for life.

3

Advice for Clinicians Working With Perpetrators

Tough and Tender

Through our experience, we have developed what we call a "tough and tender" technique. It is important to balance toughness with tenderness so that the perpetrators understand that we empathize and feel a degree of tenderness concerning their pain, losses, and separation. Generally speaking, perpetrators are people who have experienced misunderstanding or careless disregard most of their lives. Therefore, in order to gain trust and access to the perpetrators' abuse history in enough detail to be helpful in changing that behavior, you need to genuinely empathize with their experience. On the other hand, it is imperative that you take away their defensive power and control, confronting them with the realistic results and consequences of their abusive behavior. At workshops, when we play tapes of actual therapy sessions, this technique is often criticized as "awfully tough." Surprisingly enough, when rehabilitation is well underway, the perpetrators have been known to remark that they "needed someone to be tough" with them to help them differentiate between *being bad* and *behaving badly*. That is what the tough and tender tactics are intended to accomplish: to be tough on the behavior, but tender enough to heal some of the damage of the past and rebuild behavior patterns and ego structure in ways that extricate the perpetrator from being a likely candidate for repeated offense.

Before disclosure, the perpetrator in one way or another controlled the relationship with the victim. After disclosure, this sense of control is reinforced as a line of defense against shame, humiliation, defeat, further intervention, and ultimate destruction. In order to keep you, the worker, at bay, the perpetrator may attempt to control your interaction as well. It is essential that the worker *take control and keep it*, sending a clear message to the perpetrator that you mean business and that you expect full cooperation. If the perpetrator maintains control, you may not be able to intervene at all. Remember also that in incestuous families in which a "family fortress" has existed, often the abuser has called all the shots and the nonabusing parent has relinquished any control. The nonabusing parent may still love the abusing parent and may want more than ever to "pull in the drawbridge" and fortify the family ramparts against the intruder—you! If the abusing parent has family support in retaining control, your job of finding a way into the system to obtain a confession and to ensure the protection of the victim will be even more difficult.

First contact with the abuse does not always occur immediately. If your first contact with the perpetrator is in a mandated or confined facility or program, the task of structuring the relationship will be facilitated by the conditions of the institutional setting. In jail, inmates have little autonomy; they are cut off from family support and protection and are forced to comply to a complex set of rules, regulations, and authority relationships. There are known and harsh sanctions for failure to recognize and obey people of authority—and you are in a position of authority. That power balance can be used to your advantage, but needs to be monitored to ensure that it is not being abused. In a hospital or community-based institution, there is a less-apparent imbalance of power, but it exists nonetheless in the doctor-patient relationship and in the therapist-client relationship. It is still critical, even in these settings and at a time later on in the legal process, that the perpetrator confess and express guilt.

Immediate Issues: Crisis Intervention

Often when we are called upon to make an assessment and intervene, the offender has already been interviewed by the police and has bolstered up defenses to a nearly impenetrable magnitude. Human service workers should not immediately confront the perpetrator at this point of low self-esteem, fear, overwhelming guilt, defensiveness, and confusion. Instead, approach the offender with tenderness, understanding, and hope, allowing defenses to come down. Be honest with the perpetrator about what you are there to accomplish, where your loyalties are, and what are the options as well as the consequences of the abusive behavior for both offender and victim. Set up a tough and tender trust relationship that begins the treatment process with the first contact.

What to Expect

From the moment you walk into a situation such as this, the emotional climate is dominated by the simple fact that there has been an accusation of improper sexual conduct within a family system, meaning that this family has been plunged into crisis. At the worst you can expect chaos, at best reluctant cooperation. Whether you are a cleric, counselor, confidant, or case worker, your contact with the family may be the first contact since the allegation was made. If your experience with the family indicates that they may resort to violence under crisis circumstances, it is advisable to provide yourself an escort—perhaps a police escort. Should you feel the necessity for a police escort, explain to the escorting officers that you have had previous experience with the family and need their assistance as a back-up should things get out of control. Ask the officer to permit you to interview the perpetrator alone before any intervention. If you walk into an already chaotic situation with a uniformed police officer and a "pistol-drawn" attitude, it may alienate the family and prevent disclosure on the part of the perpetrator. If you have never worked with this family, prepare yourself for the worst and hope for the best.

Initial Interview With the Perpetrator After the Victim Discloses

First and foremost, it is important to remember that if you can enable the perpetrator to confess, you have already helped the victim. When the perpetrator admits the abuse, the non-abusing parent may have a tendency to believe the child more readily than if the perpetrator were to deny the abuse. Remember that the nonabusing parent probably loves both offender and victim and may have confused or divided loyalties. Imagine how wrenching it must be to hear that someone you love and trust has abused your child! Also, more important, if the perpetrator confesses, the child need not testify in court. (Remember, we need to be careful not to subject the child to additional trauma and abuse at the hands of the legal system. Our purpose is to protect the child.)

If you had previously developed a relationship with the family, you will probably be able to interview the perpetrator before the arrest. Either way, it is imperative to use a tough, direct, confrontational style regarding the allegations, making it clear that you believe the child. Because the perpetrator has been focused on getting his or her needs met rather than considering the needs of the child, the full impact of the abuse on the child may not be understood. It is absolutely necessary to clarify the emotional and physical damage the child has sustained. If necessary, read the offender excerpts from a study, a book, or an article that authoritatively enumerates the effects of incest on a child. It is essential to use the tender technique by explaining that you understand the offender's guilt and fear of family loss, but that the child's healing begins with the perpetrator's apology and that counseling can provide hope. It is necessary that you explain and prepare for police involvement and explain that you have no control over the legal proceedings, but that if the offender confesses incest, takes responsibility for it, and actively participates in a treatment program, you will be willing to recommend probation and counseling. (Be careful to suggest probation only when you have assessed the situation and diagnosed the offender as regressed. Be cautious in giving assurances when dealing with a fixated offender, a repeat offender, a rapist, or a sociopath. Incarceration may be a necessary part of rehabilitation for this type of offender. Don't make promises you can't keep!)

Once the perpetrator has confessed, recommend that a lawyer be retained. We do not recommend that you facilitate contact with an attorney. Therapeutically, it is important that the perpetrator begins here to take responsibility for the crime and for arranging for a defense. In our experience, most attorneys do not want the alleged perpetrator to admit guilt. If the initial interview was a success, the perpetrator will already have confessed and will have gained an understanding of the importance of maintaining a confession of guilt for the benefit of the victim.

If the perpetrator is remorseful, this is a good time to bring in any family members who may be present and explain the situation to them, allowing them to hear the perpetrator's admission of guilt. Make sure you provide maximum support for the family members at this time. While it will in ways be a relief to the victim to hear the perpetrator take the full burden of guilt, it will also be a highly charged moment. The victim may be pushed to emotional extremes. Siblings may also disclose, may react with relief, with anger, or with disbelief, and may even turn on the child victim and insist the perpetrator is wrongfully accused. The nonabusing parent may be caught in a terrible dilemma of choosing to believe either the child or partner, thereby seeming to abandon the other. The nonabusing parent may refuse to believe either one of them and respond with hostility, with withdrawal from the overwhelming nature of the situation, with denial, or with emotional collapse. Any of the family members may turn on you as the cause of the entire situation. Stand your ground and trust your instincts and your professional objectivity. Early therapeutic intervention enables the family to begin their grieving process and have mutual support in addition to the support of the worker while they sort through some of their immediate feelings. In terms of legal evidence, it is also helpful to have witnesses to the confession.

After the initial introductions, you will want to interview the perpetrator alone. In the following example of an initial interview, the perpetrator had called the office and asked for an appointment as soon as possible. Hearing the urgency in his voice, I asked about the nature of his concern. He briefly told me that he had been charged with sexual abuse. I set the appointment up for that evening. Here is a shortened version of this initial interview:

Counselor: Dan, you told me on the phone that you have been charged with sexually abusing your seven-year-old daughter. Can you tell me what has happened to this point?

Client: Well, Friday night a police officer and a child protection worker knocked on our door and asked if they could speak with us. My wife and I were afraid that something had happened to our girls, because they were late coming home from school. The child protection worker told us that our daughter Diana had told a friend that I had been touching her. The friend told a teacher, and then the principal at the school called the authorities. Anyway, they informed us that they had placed the girls in foster care for the weekend, to give my wife and I time to think about what we were going to do. I got angry and said that that was ridiculous, I would never hurt my child, and they informed me that they believed my daughter and that I was under arrest and would have to go with them to the police station. They told my wife that they would be back on Monday to talk further with us. After they booked me, I called my wife to bail me out and she called my mother and told her that she would have to bail me out. Anyway, I went back home with my wife and tried to talk with her. My wife has been in bed all weekend and has not spoken to me at all. I'm really worried about her, all she's done is cry and she won't talk to anyone.

Counselor: Dan, did you admit your guilt in your statement at the police station?

Client: No, like I told you before, I wouldn't ever hurt my child. I didn't do it.

Counselor: Why do you suppose Diana told her friend that you had touched her?

Client: Well, she was mad at me that morning because she couldn't spend the weekend with her grandmother.

Counselor: Dan, I know that you're really scared and hurt right now, but there are a few things that I need to tell you before we talk about the situation at home with your wife. You told me when you called on the phone that you had been charged with sexually abusing your daughter. I also know that this is an agonizing and painful time for your family. I'd like to tell you from my experience though, that you will inflict more pain and harm on your family by denying the offense than you would if you admitted your guilt.

Client: (interrupting me) I told you, I didn't do it and I'm not going to listen to this.

Counselor: That's certainly your choice and you can leave right now if you want, but maybe you ought to hear me out before you go. You're paying for the session anyway. It can't hurt to listen, and maybe I can help you and your family. What we have found is that children don't lie about abuse. Diana is only seven years old and would have no way of making up the story she told. She is too young to know what sex is. She would have had to have an adult "teach her." Through our experience, we have found out that the child can be scarred for the rest of her life if this situation goes without intervention. She'll grow up feeling that she's damaged, dirty, no good. She may turn to drugs, alcohol, or prostitution, or she may choose never to marry because of the sexual "duties" that come with marriage. I see women like this all the time in therapy, Dan. You wouldn't believe how they suffer, all because they think somehow it's their fault. If, on the other hand, Dad admits his guilt and tells his daughter that it was his fault, not hers, the child's healing can begin.

Client: Like I told you, I didn't do it.

Counselor: I'll tell you the truth Dan, if I had sexually abused my child, I would be afraid to admit it too. It's real scary not knowing what is going to happen and knowing that you may lose your wife and children if anyone finds out it's true. On the other hand, you can help your daughter and your family begin to heal, and we can help you to use more appropriate behavior with your children from now on. I know that for you to have resorted to getting sexual gratification with your child, you must have been hurting terribly, feeling confused and desperate. We can work on those issues together Dan, and help you become whole again. At the same time, Diana could be helped to realize that Daddy made a terrible mistake and that she isn't to blame in any way. If you admit that you did inappropriately touch Diana, I will intervene for you and do what I can to minimize the damage to you and your family. Dan, we're talking about *the rest of Diana's life* being affected. If you continue to deny the offense, and an investigation is done, and they find the allegations founded, you're going to be in a lot more trouble than if you admit your guilt and commit to getting some help. There is help available Dan, but you have to take responsibility for what you've done.

Client: If I did tell you that some of it was true, what would happen? I'm not saying that I did do anything, I'm just asking.

Counselor: Well, the first thing we would need to do is talk about the abuse in detail and find out why you did what you did. We would need to let the authorities know, and your wife. If everything goes well, you and I would get to know each other very well and would see each other every week for a long time. Dan, did you touch Diana in a sexual way?

Client: (barely audible) I touched her, but I didn't hurt her.

Counselor: I know you didn't intend to hurt her. But you are her Daddy and she trusted you to protect her, not make hurtful demands on her.

Client: I just wanted someone to love me.

Counselor: And there's no doubt in my mind that Diana loves you, Dan. I can see that in the way you relate to each other. But you know there is a difference between the way in which an adult man and a woman love each other and the way a parent and a child love each other. The reason Diana told someone at school what was happening to her was that she is scared to death and very confused. She knows she loves you, but she also knows that other Dads and daughters don't love each other physically the way you and she have. She senses something is wrong about that. And she is terrified that she's the one who has done something wrong, and that she'll be punished by losing your love. You see Dan, she's in a terrible bind right now. Who does she protect: herself, or you? She has finally made the decision that she has to take care of herself. And she is right to do that. As her father, you are more than capable of taking care of yourself. Right now she needs to know she made the right choice. She needs to know that she did nothing wrong. She needs to know she has nothing to feel guilty about or ashamed of. The police are involved now. To Diana that is proof positive that somebody has done something wrong. It's up to you to clarify for her where the wrong is. Are you going to let her continue to think she's the one who is wrong—that there is something wrong with her? Or are you going to let her off the hook and tell her the truth? Do you love her enough to set her free of the blame? Or are you going to let her suffer over it for the rest of her life?

Client: (crying) I love my daughter.

Counselor: The choice is yours, Dan. You say you love your daughter. Do you love her enough to do that for her? She needs to hear you say it, Dan. Can you do that for Diana?

Client: She's only seven years old, and this will blow over and she'll never remember any of this. I love her more than most fathers and she knows that. I didn't do anything to hurt her. Social Services and the school are just trying to make trouble for us. The way people are now, you can't even hug your child without someone being suspicious. I'm going to hire an attorney and sue everybody involved so that they can't do this to another family.

Counselor: I know you didn't mean to hurt Diana, Dan, but sometimes the hurt doesn't show on the outside. It isn't until later when the damage is apparent. If Diana's love is so important to you, then you better think about the price of your denial. She'll end up hating you and the damage could be irreparable. If you really love her the way you'd like me to believe, then why is it I'm getting the feeling that your safety is more important than hers? Something you should realize is that this is going to go to court anyway, now, and Diana is going to have to talk about this in court. Can you imagine how hard that could be on her?

Client: Court? How can they take a seven-year-old little girl's word against mine? They can't prove anything.

Counselor: (with notable changes in demeanor and style) You know Dan, I'm really feeling very angry with you. A while ago you asked a hypothetical question about what would happen if you did admit your guilt. I thought then that you were really ready to assume responsibility for what you did. I believed that you love Diana and didn't want to hurt her. Now I'm not so sure. You continue to deny and be evasive and you are also choosing to ignore the damage that Diana has experienced and will continue to experience. You can deny this the rest of your life Dan, and there's nothing anybody can do to change your mind, but I will not continue to work with you. There are too many people who want help and are ready to make some changes in their lives. My heart is breaking for Diana. She's only a little girl and she's the one being sentenced to life in prison. I guess there's nothing more that I can say, Dan. I believe Diana. And you know the price Diana will pay for your silence. My suggestion to you is to get a good attorney.

Client: Are you telling me that I can't come back?

Counselor: No, you may come back at any time you're willing to work.

Client: I'm so afraid they'll put me in jail. I couldn't survive that.

Counselor: But you're ready to "lock up" the life of your seven year old? (softening: speaking nearly in a whisper, tilting head slightly, leaning forward confidentially, and reaching out with one hand as if to touch his arm) Dan, did you abuse Diana?

Client: (head down, speaking in a choked whisper) I didn't abuse her. I might have touched her. It might have scared her.

Counselor: "Might have?"

Client: Okay I did, but I didn't hurt her. She's my daughter! I wouldn't hurt her.

Counselor: (gently yet firmly; spoken very softly) How did you touch her, Dan?

Client: It was just once. I reached out to hug her and my hand touched her chest.

Counselor: I see. Then you did touch her breast like she said?

Client: (almost inaudibly) Once. (then angrily) I didn't fuck her for God's sake! What do you want me to say?

Counselor: I want you to tell the truth.

At this point in therapy, continue to build rapport with the client and be very nonjudgmental and encouraging. Reiterate that there is hope for healing for the whole family. Suggest that an attorney be retained, but explain that the attorney may suggest the perpetrator continue to deny the charges (some attorneys do not want their clients to sign a statement of guilt), and emphasize again how important it is that the perpetrator assume responsibility for the abuse. Start rebuilding the perpetrator's self-esteem by explaining how right it was to tell the truth, and offer to assist the family by writing a letter of recommendation, but not until you have met every week for one hour sessions for a few weeks. Remember, it is important to know all the facts before making an assessment or recommendation concerning incarceration. In this particular case, I suggested that Dan find a place to live so that the girls could go back home with their mother, which would help her and also help the children. Dan was anxious to tell Diana how sorry he was and to make restitution for what he had done. I suggested that he talk to the caseworker assigned to Diana's case to see if he would be permitted to send her cards or short letters. We also talked about the effects of all that had happened on his wife and tried to imagine what she may be feeling. It was very enlightening for Dan to imagine what his wife might have been experiencing. He sobbed through the remainder of the session, saying that he had "done it now" and that he would lose his family. I asked him if he would mind if I called his wife and asked her to come in. He said he would not mind and that he would pay for her counseling as well as the girls'. Dan did not end up going to jail. He continued coming for weekly counseling for a little over a year. He never cancelled an appointment or harassed his wife or children. The court forbid him from seeing his wife or children for one year or until I felt it was appropriate. Dan's wife had a nervous breakdown and required hospitalization for a two-week period, was medicated, and continued in therapy with me. She and Dan decided to reconcile when she realized she still loved him and wanted their family to be reunited. Joint therapy followed for about twelve weeks around reunification and marital issues. Family therapy followed that to prepare the way for Dan's return to the household. At this time, Diana appears to be doing extremely well and appears to be happy and adjusted. Dan was placed on three years' probation and continues to see me every six weeks for what we call a "tune-up."

Who Leaves?

It is our contention that because the perpetrator is charged with responsibility for sexual abuse, the child and family should not be punished by being removed from all that is familiar and comforting in the critical and extremely painful period following disclosure. It is essential that the child be surrounded with support, familiarity, and as much comfort as possible once the disclosure has been made. Children do not have the ego strength to withstand the kind of denial that occurs in most families on the part of the perpetrator who now realizes the legal implications of the offense, the nonabusing parent who feels torn between the story of the child and the story of the spouse and wracked with guilt that something like this might have been occurring without even sensing it, and the siblings and extended family members who want to protect themselves from personal and public exposure. There is likely to be a great deal of blaming, and many are likely to cast doubt on the credibility of the child's story. The child will often feel attacked and disbelieved by all those held most dear and trustworthy and will need the comfort of familiarity in this chaotic time. Removing the child from home at this point would send a message of punishment. Isn't it true that we are advised that responsible punishment is to remove privileges from our children when they make mistakes? So how bad must this "mistake" have been if everything the child values is removed at the same time?

Removing the perpetrator from the home sends an entirely different message. The perpetrator is an adult, a person much more capable than a child of processing this crisis, of adjusting to a changed environment, of seeking support. If we are serious about placing the responsibility for the offense with the offender, we must be sure to be consistent. We must be careful to allow the perpetrator to shoulder the responsibility rather than to place it on the child. We must begin here to break the power cycle of the perpetrator, to give the child some of the power needed to begin healing, and to give the child a message of support, belief, and protection.

In summary, we support making the decision about who leaves in the following order of preference:

1. Arrange to remove the perpetrator from the home.
2. Arrange to remove the nonabusing parent and the child(ren) to a safe place until the perpetrator can be removed.
3. Arrange to remove the child to the custody of a trusted person known to the victim who can be trusted to console and protect the victim.
4. Arrange to remove the child to a secure shelter where consistent contact with a care-giving adult can be sustained, preferably where there can be therapeutic contact with other child victims of similar age, where treatment can begin immediately, and where the child can visit with supportive family members in a supervised setting.

The focus needs to be on the emotional and physical needs of the child when we are planning for separation of family members to protect the safety of the victim.

Long-Term Treatment Issues

Assuming Responsibility

Let us hypothesize that a man calls you for an appointment "as soon as possible." When you ask him the nature of his concern, he states that he has a personal problem to discuss with you. You schedule an appointment, and he comes in for his initial session. During the course of the counseling session, he informs you that he is waiting to go to court on a sexual abuse charge. Your first task is still to enable him to assume responsibility for his crime.

Follow the same steps you would if you knew beforehand that he is accused of a sexual crime; even if he has told his attorney and the police that he did not do it. Use the tough and tender approach; appeal to him for the healing of his child and for appropriate placement of the inappropriate guilt victims experience when the perpetrator denies the crime. Offer to help him through the disclosure with the police and the family, and reinforce that you respect him for admitting his guilt. The most important thing to remember is that the primary objective for the offender is to *assume responsibility for the crime.*

Shame

We all feel shame. Whether we were shamed as children for wetting the bed or as adults for making a choice that proved harmful to someone else or to someone's self-esteem, we all have experiences with shame. In order to more fully understand the importance of shame as a therapeutic issue when working with perpetrators, try an exercise we use in our workshops. Start with a relaxation exercise designed to relax the body and clear the mind, then:

> ... for just a moment, let yourself get in touch with one of the areas of shame in your life. Spend a moment or two allowing that feeling of shame to become real in the present. Allow it to fill your body, knowing that you will shrug it off again in a few moments. Allow your body to move with it, respond to it, reflect it. Without saying a word to yourself, explore the shame and let it be part of this moment. As you allow it to come out of the past and into the present, allow your body to respond as it chooses—and be aware of what happens. Allow it to dominate you for a moment. Let your body express the shame you feel. Act it out. Once you are fully in touch with the shame, put it back where it belongs. Be gentle with yourself and forgive yourself for whatever caused it, knowing that you are an adult now and have moved beyond it. Put it back in the past where it belongs and allow yourself to return to the present at the point where you departed.

Now, what was the experience like for you? How did your body respond to the feeling of shame? What happened to your head, your neck, your shoulders, your eyes and face, your posture? If the experience was similar to that of others who have tried it, you found yourself shriveling up, drawing inward, trying to hide from the world. Now imagine being so filled with shame that you needed to stay shriveled up all the time. Many of the perpetrators we have worked with are either shriveled up with shame or the opposite— fortified against absorbing any more shame by layer after layer of false bravado; sometimes they even have themselves fooled into believing they are safe.

In her workshops on working with adult victim-survivors, Mary Louise Wise presents a Cycle of Internalized Shame inspired by the work of Gershen Kaufman, which we find equally applicable to the perpetrator who was once a victim. We have been inspired by both models and have made further modifications to meet our own needs. Figure 3–1 presents our version of the cycle by which individuals move from accepting a shame identity from external sources to internalizing that shame and reinforcing that shamefulness as the core of their identity.

The cycle begins with the caretaker. When the caretaker is unavailable (as in the case of an emotionally inaccessible caretaker, a physically unavailable caretaker, an alcohol or substance abuser, an overburdened parent, or an institutionalized parent), an incapable caretaker (as in the case of a very young parent who lacks parenting ability or a parent who may lack the physical or emotional skills necessary to parenting), or an unwilling caretaker (as in the case of a neglectful caretaker or a physically, emotionally, or sexually abusive caretaker), unable to nurture the child, the developmentally egocentric child gets a message of guilt: "I've done something wrong. There must be something wrong with me, otherwise Daddy and Mommy would take care of me." This child continues to develop with the underlying conviction that he or she is flawed in some way, and begins to look to the environment for confirmation of that flaw. That, in turn, produces anxiety in the child. Next, the child develops defenses to protect himself or herself against absorbing any more shame. You are familiar with the ego defenses: withdrawal, acting-out, aggression, hyperactivity, self-consciousness, supercritical evaluation of others, denial, avoidance, and overachievement, to name a few. The defenses allow the child either to maintain outward distance between himself or herself and potentially shaming or blaming others, or to focus inward, becoming hypervigilant of self in order to monitor potentially shameful behavior before it occurs. The social distance produced by the defenses reinforces the message that the child is guilty of something so terrible that no one wants to be close, only now it feels more like shame.

Convinced that he or she is "bad," the child begins to behave like a bad person by acting out. Acting out may take the form of juvenile or adult delinquency, breaking rules, defying authority, bizarre appearance or behavior, "crazy" behavior, depression, extreme withdrawal, hostility against others, or self-destructive behavior such as overuse of drugs, alcohol, or sex. The message that goes along with the behavior is: "I'm a bad person. I do bad things." When things get out of hand and no other correction is forthcoming, society steps in to try to draw this person's behavior back within limits by imposing social and legal sanctions, family disapproval, social disapproval, psychiatric intervention, efforts to force behavior change. The accompanying message is: "I'm a bad person. I do bad things. You tell me I'm bad. I must be bad." After a few trips around this circle of progressive reinforcement, the child internalizes the messages, confirming the original hypothesis: "I'm guilty. There *is* something wrong with me," until it translates: "I'm bad. Everyone agrees I'm bad. So we all concur, I'm a bad person who is always doing bad things."

When I demonstrate this cycle with a client as a cognitive tool, clients are surprised when I direct their attention back to the beginning of the cycle:

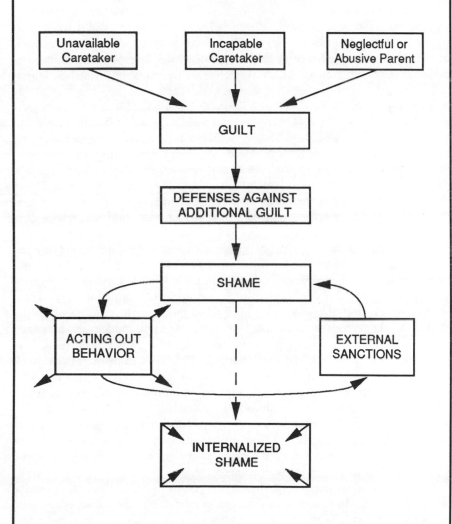

Figure 3-1

THE CYCLE OF INTERNALIZED SHAME

| Unavailable Caretaker | Incapable Caretaker | Neglectful or Abusive Parent |

GUILT

DEFENSES AGAINST ADDITIONAL GUILT

SHAME

ACTING OUT BEHAVIOR

EXTERNAL SANCTIONS

INTERNALIZED SHAME

Adapted from the work of Gershen Kaufman, *Shame: The Power of Caring,* 1980, Schenkman Books, Inc., and from Dr. Mary Louise Wise.

the process does not start with the child, it starts with the caretaker. Often I see a light go on at that point: "Oh. Maybe I'm O.K. after all. Maybe there was something wrong with the people who were supposed to be my caretakers. Maybe it's not all my fault." Convincing them that they are not all bad is an enormous task, but one that must be undertaken for all parties involved in an abusive situation.

As a sidelight, and to underscore how easy it is to start the cycle of internalized shame into motion, allow me to replay a personal anecdote. A parent who was a professional trained in child development had a preschool-age child who was a handful, to put it mildly. Because of her training, she believed she could control the child's behavior by reasoning with her daughter, failing to acknowledge that young children do not become reasonable beings until they reach a specific developmental level. This child had not yet reached the age of reason. Of course, the child's favorite time for acting out was when she was in public with her mother, a time when the mother's efforts to control the child with reason would be taxed to the limit. Sometimes, in utter frustration, this mother would look down at her daughter and say, "Oh Martha. You were just born bad!" Nonmaliciously in this case—out of her own frustration—the parent was giving the child the clearest message that there was something wrong with her, and already the child was responding with aggressive acting-out behavior.

When we step through a process such as we have done in introducing the Cycle of Internalized Shame, we are tempted to limit our thinking to the child victim as we conceptualize each stage. After all, it most certainly applies to victims. But now take a conceptual leap and apply it to an adult perpetrator who once *was* that abused child. Recall for a moment the description of the W.A.R. Cycle in chapter 2, and look for ways these two models enhance each other. The abused child progresses to become the shameful adult who acts out shame and "badness" against another child. This adult may, because of the developmental deficiencies of childhood, be acting out on an emotional level against a perceived peer. These connections are made not to excuse the adult—nothing can excuse the abuses of power and trust that occur when an adult abuses a child—but it does make the whole baffling mess a little more understandable. Perhaps if you can understand it, you can come to a point where you, as a person outside the experience, can reach in to help lead the way out for those caught up within the cycle.

The physical expression of shame we got in touch with in the exercise we asked you to do earlier is usually obvious in the perpetrators who come to us for treatment. While not all symptoms are evident in every perpetrator, several of them usually are. Especially among incarcerated perpetrators, there is usually difficulty in making and sustaining eye contact; the perpetrator may appear slouched with head and neck drawn into the shoulders; posture may be poor as if hunched over to protect the internal organs, or upright and rigid as though wearing body armor; some are disheveled, others are super-fastidious about their appearance; some are very quiet and withdrawn, others are almost hyperactive and agitated; some are so devoid of self-esteem that they make no effort to defend themselves, others want to take over and put the worker and everyone else on the defensive; some are able to relate no significant achievements from the entire course of their lives, others will rattle off an impressive list of achievements; some seem to want to blend in with the walls and disappear, others try very hard to command attention and to overpower everyone they encounter. Looking back at the partial list of defenses we generated a few paragraphs ago, you may be able to see how you might look at the way in which the perpetrator presents and, from that, speculate fairly accurately about his or her preferred mode of defense. Therapeutically you would deal differentially with opposing ends of the spectrum. The withdrawn perpetrator needs abundant reinforcement and support in order to acquire sufficient ego strength to begin to value rehabilitation. In contrast, you need to confront and strip away the defensiveness of the acting-out perpetrator, before the pain and vulnerability can be approached; then the same ego strength building needs to occur in an effort to convince the perpetrator to want to change.

Leon Festinger developed the concept of *cognitive dissonance,* emotional discomfort that occurs when an individual violates his or her own values or beliefs. If a person believes he is bad, he will find bad behavior in himself and others to be consonant with that belief: "I am a bad person. I do bad things,"—no dissonance, no reason to make a change. One means of intervention is to *create* cognitive dissonance in order to promote change. If a person believes he is good, he will experience considerable discomfort from the dissonance that is set up when he behaves badly: "I am a good person. I do bad things." Somehow or another, the individual will have to change either the self-concept or the behavior in order to reduce the dissonance. Our objective is to change the behavior. In order to render the behavior change permanent and to support changed behavior, the self-concept must change concurrently. Sometimes it is a long reach to find a place to start when working with an individual whose self-esteem has been so damaged by internalized shame, but once you can identify one area of goodness or strength in the perpetrator's life, you can build on that, working toward cognitively restructuring the self-concept: "I am a good person. I do good things." Once the perpetrator internalizes goodness in place of shame, we are on our way to preventing repeated offense. Cognitive restructuring will result in the perpetrator being less likely to resume destructive behavior.

Self-Esteem

If a person values himself, he is likely to value others as well. If a person has no sense of value, no positive sense of self-esteem, it is likely that he will see no value in others either. As Sid Simon, author, lecturer, workshop designer and leader, and professor of Psychological Education at the University of Massachusetts says, "People who like themselves don't hurt themselves or anyone else." Sid and Suzanne Simon (noted writer, lecturer, workshop designer and presenter, and therapist specializing in work with incest victims, sexual abuse, and adult incest survivors) travel the country lecturing and presenting workshops on a broad spectrum of human relations topics. They have developed Six Conditions for the Nurture of Self-Esteem that we have found helpful in working with perpetrators. We have adapted their model for work with perpetrators.

We know that one of the effects of sexual victimization is distorted self-esteem. For perpetrators of sexual victimization who were victimized themselves, there is a double dose of distorted self-esteem. In our examination of the process of internalizing shame (figure 3–1) we saw how the self-esteem of the abused or neglected child is shaped by the egocentric childhood messages of self-blame the child takes from the abuse or neglect. Later these messages are internalized and sustained by a cycle of reinforcement: "I'm bad. I do bad things. You say I'm bad. So I must be bad. Bad people do bad things," and on and on, around and around the cycle of reinforcement. For some abused or neglected children turned adults, the ultimate "bad" is the abuse of their own child. We see this principle operating in the W.A.R. Cycle presented in figure 2–1. If we are satisfied that the perpetrator experiences social sanctions alone (imprisonment) *without* treatment to interrupt these cycles, we can hardly expect a permanent change in behavior. We may call our prisons "correctional institutions," but very few of them offer corrective treatment beyond the rigid structure and behavior modification of the prison environment. Little of that directly addresses the roots of the problem of incestuous behavior. One of the critical points of intervention must be the perpetrator's self-esteem. Whether the perpetrator is incarcerated or not, the improvement of self-esteem will result in greater self-respect which will likely result in respect and value of others. The perpetrator's increase in self-esteem translates to a decreased risk of recidivism.

According to the Simons', the following six conditions are required for self-esteem to be established and maintained:

1. *Engagement With Risk.* Willingness for and experience with risk-taking increases self-esteem. Areas for engagement are physical risk, spiritual risk, intellectual risk, and emotional risk. We need to test ourselves to learn "what we are made of." We need to find our limits and to challenge those limits in order to keep ourselves growing. That means we need to risk failure in order to reach for mastery. The person who spends a lifetime sitting at home for fear of being injured while moving around in the world is crippled by that fear. That person needs to risk the injury in order to explore the world and to learn from it. The person who is satisfied with a second-grade understand-

ing of spirituality in order to maintain a sense of security is limited by a false sense of security. That person needs to take some spiritual risks to challenge his own understanding and to risk learning something that will provide a more comprehensive understanding. We need to take intellectual risks by changing our patterns of absorbing intellectual material. Those of us who spend our time watching the kinds of programming typical of commercial television need to risk reading a good book, or taking a course, or attending a lecture in order to switch our minds to other channels. Those of us who live in isolation from fear of being hurt in a relationship need to risk intimacy with another in order to challenge the limits of loving and to allow ourselves to risk being loved.

For the perpetrator, emotional risk is extremely dangerous. Perpetrators often turn to their own children as sexual partners in order to avoid the emotional risk of confronting their age-mate partner or in order to avoid leaving the relationship to establish a more satisfying one, or even to avoid looking for another age-mate partner as an alternative to an unhappy relationship. It is fair to generalize that most perpetrators are *stuck* emotionally. They have drawn inward for protection, looking to get their physical and emotional needs met within the relative safety of their own families. Part of the work of therapy is to help perpetrators engage in risks of all kinds, to test themselves in the world, and to establish limits and options.

2. Models and Mentors. If we are to gain in self-esteem, we need to have someone to show us how to be successful people. We all need someone in our lives who does what we do (or want to do) a little better than we are able to do it at any given time. While we learn sensually by watching, reading, and hearing, we learn most effectively by hands-on experience; we call it *operational learning*. Children learn more from doing things with us than from hearing us tell them what we did or what we should do. Given the choice between absorbing what we say and what we do, our children absorb what we do. So it is with adult relationships as well. We learn more enduringly from what we see and what we actually operate on than from anything else. Having someone in our lives who shows us how, who does it with us, who does it while we watch, then gives us some guidance as we do it ourselves is invaluable to our learning. *Models* can be people we imitate: Jesus Christ, Mohandas Gandhi, Mother Theresa, Eleanor Roosevelt—people who are unavailable to us physically, but serve as models of what we would like to be. *Mentors* are teachers who are available to us: the senior worker in your department, Mom and Dad, the coach of your team, the president of your organization, the next-door neighbor who is so good at what you would like to be able to do, the teacher who makes vastly complicated tasks seem so easy to accomplish by showing you how. These are all people who serve as patterns for possibility and help us to reach for it.

Look for a moment at the kinds of models and mentors most perpetrators have: the perpetrator probably learned abusive behavior from abusive models and mentors! Here, the therapeutic challenge is to point out the flaws in the perpetrator's models and mentors and to assist in a search for more appropriate, growth inducing, healthy models and mentors. Therapy may be the first circumstance in which the perpetrator has been allowed to dream. You, the therapist, may be the first healthy mentor. That is a lot of responsibility to take upon yourself—and you do take it upon yourself for a while. But your job is to eventually help the perpetrator function in the world again, without you. Part of your job is going to have to be to help find appropriate others who can represent patterns of behavior that will be constructive rather than destructive. One of the ways we accomplish this task is by monitoring the perpetrator's sociogram, updating it as new people and connections enter the picture, and working toward strengthening healthy relationships. We encourage perpetrators to take risks—and then reward their efforts. We train them to look for growth and strength in every new experience and to begin to change their orientation from a protective one ("I'll never try that again") to what Dr. Susan Jeffers refers to in her book, *Feel the Fear and Do It Anyway,* as a position of power: ("Wow! I can experience failure without being destroyed by it!").

Most of the perpetrators we have dealt with have been indicted rather than confirmed by the adults in their lives. They have learned from critical others that they are incompetent, that they cannot handle their own experiences successfully, and that they had better protect themselves from experience because they are inadequate to deal with it. So, in therapy, a great deal of retraining needs to take place. As therapists, we need to take over (temporarily) the role of the competent parent and teach perpetrators to risk, to learn from their experiences, to know that they are competent people capable of making responsible choices, people capable of learning and growing and changing their way of relating to the world. Once they truly know they are capable, they have taken a giant step toward self-empowerment.

3. *Empowerment.* Empowerment refers to one's own power over one's self. It is the power to control and manage one's own life. It is the power to make one's own decisions and to assume responsibility for the consequences of those decisions. It is the power to determine what is of value to one's self and to live one's life in accordance with those values. Values clarification work is enormously helpful in sorting out those aspects of life that are truly of value to an individual and in assisting to direct one's energy toward living out those values. As people make decisions for themselves based on what they value, take charge of their own lives, and set their own life courses, self-esteem increases.

By now you can imagine how important this is for perpetrators who have blamed their victims or other innocent parties for their behavior. They always believed they had no choices, no power. They were "forced" to do what they did to the child; forced by previous learning, by "circumstances," by the alcohol, by destiny, or any of a number of other people or things. That attitude cannot be tolerated and must be confronted head on. Perpetrators must be made to see that they always have choices and that *they* decide what to do, even if by deciding not to decide! Therapy must seek ways to empower perpetrators to take control of their own lives, including taking responsibility for their behavior. Work must then proceed toward developing a system of priorities or values that will guide their choice-making. This work is ongoing. It is a process of filling up an empty space with something healthy and constructive. If perpetrators are to resist the cognitive dissonance inevitable in making life changes, dissonance that will strongly pull them back to their old ways of behaving, they need to be constantly reminded of where they are going and what the rewards of that journey will be. For the perpetrator, the rewards are the hope of healed and improved relationships and taking and maintaining control of one's own life.

Yet, sometimes the damage a perpetrator has undergone before seeking counseling is too great to be repaired. Sometimes the client is not motivated enough to make such drastic life changes—or is too scared or too defensive. But we can try. In fact, we will go so far as to say that we *must* try. The price is too great if we do not try: damaged people living in damaged families and damaged communities where there is no way out of the cycle of pain. Society steps in and takes over by removing the perpetrator to a prison. We can disconnect a perpetrator from family, child from parent, spouse from spouse, and on down the line, leaving the injured parties to deal with a continuing cycle of disconnection and dysfunction.

4. Connectedness. We all need to belong. We all need to be connected with someone or something. Most of us need to be connected to our family of origin, our family of creation, our workplace, our racial and ethnic background, and to the people, environment, and institutions around us. When we lose connection, we lose our sense of value and purpose in the world, and we lose our frame of reference. When we fail to deal with disrupted connections, we become isolated and incomplete, and our self-esteem suffers.

When working with perpetrators of incest, we often see that all connectedness is gone. The family connections are severed, community connection is broken, relationships with primary loved ones are shattered, connection to workplace is interrupted, and especially if institutionalized, connection with the environment is broken and replaced with an alien and forced environment. In order to re-establish some connectedness, we need to help perpetrators reconnect with their former environment to the greatest extent possible and to connect with new environmental components that will nourish and sustain them. The therapist needs to join the perpetrator in search of answers to questions such as: Who is available as a source of connection? What sorts of relationship connections are needed? How can constructive workplace connections be made? Where can support be found? Who will be there to instill energy, and confidence? Who and what can help establish wholeness? The journey toward forgiveness holds the promise of making some reconnections, but where else in life must new connections be made? Again, the sociogram can be a helpful evaluative tool. What recreational, social, spiritual, intellectual, and emotional connections can be made? How can this person begin to build support, challenge, and affirmation into his or her life?

5. *Uniqueness.* We all need to feel special in order to have high self-esteem. Many of us first experience our uniqueness in the reflection of our parents' love. We hear them tell us that we are special, that we do certain things well, that we are loved for our freckles as well as our sensitivity, that Mom loves the way we keep the garden weeded and Dad loves the way we scramble eggs. As we become adults, other mirrors reflect our strengths. The boss loves the way we manage tough situations, the spouse loves the way we love, the kids love the way we engage them in games, and the neighbors applaud us for the leadership role we take in the community. We can get that essential sense of uniqueness from external validation or from internal validation. Internal validation happens when we are able to recognize our own strengths and validate ourselves. Therapists assist clients in self-validation by exercises such as asking a client to record in a journal all compliments he or she receives for a given period of time and then read the list to the therapist. Reality work can follow to remove the blocks that help us invalidate the validations ("He said that to be nice, not because he really meant it." "What was she supposed to say, "I think you stink"?" "I'm really not very good. I did it well by mistake that time.") Another exercise is to assist the client to identify admirable or respectable strengths in others and then transpose those that apply to himself or herself, writing them out using "I" statements: "I respect myself for. . . . I like the way I. . . . I honor my quality of. . . ."

When working with a person as disconnected as most perpetrators are, where in their lives are they going to be able to find a place where they are nurtured, affirmed, validated? Where will they find a person or a place to mirror their strengths and their specialness? How will they begin to internalize respect in a society where they have lost nearly everyone's respect—even their own? They can begin with you, the therapist. You can begin teaching them the language of validation. You can be their first uniqueness mirror. Once they get the idea, they can direct the process by validating their victims, their significant-others, their families of origin, their own perpetrator and, from there, work toward validating themselves and repairing their self-esteem so that they no longer need hurt themselves or anyone else. They need to learn to seek validation from self and others and to make connections that will foster validation and limit invalidation. Therapeutically, you can help them to identify periods in their lives when they experienced high self-esteem, what was happening in their lives that supported and maintained the self-esteem, and to build more of those positive experiences into their present patterns of relating to the world.

6. *Recognition.* If we are to maintain high self-esteem, we need the esteem of others. The whole process of internalization of a social value starts with externalized expression of that value. If you are recognized from without, you will eventually internalize that recognition. In order to do that you need to develop a sense of purpose, achievement, and productivity. Once these are in place, mechanical as they might at first seem, you will begin to earn external affirmation for your purposeful, achievement-oriented, and productive behavior, even if that affirmation is something as mechanical as a pay check! The external validation opens the way for internalized validation. Susan Jeffers has a unique way of putting it. She says that the subconscious does not know whether what we tell it is *true* or not, it just registers the input it gets. So, when we give our subconscious an "I can't, I'm a screw-up, I'm worthless" message, it registers on its tape: "WEAK . . . INCOMPE-TENT . . . WORTHLESS." The next time we need to make a choice or decision, the tape starts playing back and influences our decision. Conversely, we can begin to give our subconscious positive messages ("I can, I did well, I am of value"), the subconscious registers in its memory banks: "STRONG . . . COMPETENT . . . VALUABLE." With this kind of message playing back, a very different influence is brought to bear on our decision making. Recognition from therapists and fellow group members, when the perpetrator is encouraged to take some risks within a supportive therapeutic setting, is a first step toward replacing the old "I can't" tapes with new "I can, I did" tapes. The following is an example one author often shares in workshops, illustrating how this process can begin—sometimes serendipitously!

> While working with a group of incarcerated offenders, I decided to give the perpetrators in the group a personality inventory. This was done in an effort to gather some data to begin to determine whether there were one or more personality characteristics these men had in common that might help us develop a predictive measure of predisposition to incest perpetration. After permission was obtained from the prison authorities and from the individual group members, the California Psychological Inventory (CPI) was administered to each man. Once the results were tabulated and interpreted, I met with each man individually to explain the implications. One of the men was a member of a motorcycle gang. His hair covered his downcast eyes he never smiled, he always sat hunched over, defensively protecting his "soft spots,"

and he was unwashed, unkempt, and uncommunicative. The day he came into my office to hear the results of his CPI was "one of those days" for me. I was recovering from a cold and was still experiencing the feeling of my head being disconnected from my body. While in this haze, I proceeded to explain his scores, unwittingly interchanging the word apathy with the word empathy. He had scored high on *apathy,* but nonetheless, I went on and told him that his high score on *empathy* meant that he was really a very sensitive individual who was highly attuned to other people and cared deeply about what they were experiencing. I went on and on telling him how sensitive and caring he was. He left my office without much comment. But a changed man appeared in group from that day on. His posture straightened and we began to realize how tall he was. Gradually his hair was cut shorter and shorter and for the first time he made eye contact. He appeared neater with every group session. He began to appear in clean clothes—then shined shoes! This man had bought into my accidental (and desperately needed) validation and began to internalize it. Before long the internalized self-esteem began to show in his appearance. He began to care about himself and about other people around him. Not many months later, after an amazing amount of therapeutic progress, he was granted parole and left prison a changed man. This might never have happened if I hadn't mistaken *apathy* for *empathy* that day and perpetrated my error on that inmate. Or was it an error? Maybe it was seeing with another kind of vision.

This example is the converse of the Cycle of Internalized Shame; more like a Cycle of Internalized Self-Esteem—something most of us get from good parenting. But, for many perpetrators, positive conditions for the development and maintenance of self-esteem have *never* existed. Some will find first exposure to these conditions while they are in prison. If things get tough on the outside, it is easy enough to violate parole and return to the environment that provided the conditions for building self-esteem. We are convinced that happens. If society makes it tough enough to maintain the new self-concept that says, "I am a valuable person. I deserve to feel good about myself. Good people do good things," it is easy enough to revert to the old, "I'm a bad person who does bad things" self-concept. How do perpetrators find a sense of purpose and productivity if they cannot find a job, if no one will give them a chance? How can they gain a sense of achievement when no one in their environment is willing to get close enough to see that they have changed? It is part of our professional philosophy that one of the functions of our job is to help the individual and the family to forge a framework upon which to build self-esteem in order to protect against recidivism. If perpetrators lose their self-esteem or lose the opportunity for obtaining self-esteem, they lose the very essence of what it means to live as a human being. In therapy we can begin to teach them how to build self-esteem. One of the greatest joys of work with perpetrators is seeing self-esteem grow. One of the greatest tragedies is seeing self-esteem stagnate or die and watching the perpetrator head in the direction of continuing abuse.

Loss

When dealing with a perpetrator of an incestuous crime, you will see that there are many residual loss issues to be dealt with as well as related loss issues the family and perpetrator must deal with. The perpetrator's immediate losses often include the respect of friends; the community's sympathy; a job or business relations; the emotional support of extended family; and the right to involvement with his or her primary family. With all of these losses comes the loss of interaction with people in home, work, and community environments. In essence, a perpetrator of an incestuous crime is like a person without a country. You can see, then, how needful and vulnerable the perpetrator is likely to be to someone who approaches with firmness, tenderness, empathy, and understanding. Once such a relationship can be established, the worker can become a trusted intervenor. The perpetrator is likely to be more cooperative, less defended, and more willing to be honest. The tenderness opens the way for the toughness: together the balance of tough and tender is likely to allow maximum disclosure, maximum opportunity for intervention, and maximum therapeutic healing for the perpetrator, the victim, and the family.

Recall for a moment that according to Nicholas Groth, one of the characteristics of the regressed offender is that pedophilic behavior is a maladaptive attempt to cope with a specific stressor. Groth estimates that 80 to 85 percent of pedophilic sex offenders are of the regressed type. Using the Social Readjustment Rating Scale developed by T. H. Holmes and R. H. Rahe to list commonly experienced life changes, we can see that related to each change (or stressor) on the list is some concomitant loss. To illustrate, figure 3–2 lists the top fifteen losses in order of magnitude, coupled with a related loss possibility.

Many other possible losses may ensue from each of the life events on the scale. We provided these examples to stimulate your thinking about how even welcomed life events have a loss component, and that with each of these losses we lose a piece of ourselves that we must then refine, adjust, or redefine—a stressful endeavor in itself. If one's self-esteem is already in the basement, so to speak, a small number of these losses constitutes a disproportionately great loss of self. As a colleague once put it: "If a kid has a hundred pennies, it's no big deal if someone takes one of them: he has ninety-nine more. But if a kid has only ten pennies, it's a very big deal if someone takes one: he has only nine left!" The smaller the amount of a valuable commodity we have, the more precious each unit becomes.

Figure 3-2

LOSS EVENTS RELATED TO LIFE EVENTS

Life Event*

1. Death of a spouse
2. Divorce
3. Marital separation
4. Jail term
5. Death of a close family member
6. Personal injury or illness
7. Marriage
8. Fired at work
9. Marital reconciliation
10. Retirement
11. Change in health of family member
12. Pregnancy
13. Sex difficulties
14. Gain of new family member
15. Business readjustment

Loss Event

Loss of a life partner
Loss of dream of perfect marriage
Loss of significant relationship
Loss of contact with loved ones
Loss of supportive other
Loss of function
Loss of independence
Loss of identification with job
Loss of identity as "separated person"
Loss of time structure
Loss of familiar routine
Loss of identity as "childless"
Loss of sexual pleasure
Loss of freedom
Loss of familiarity

* Life Events are taken from the Social Readjustment Rating Scale, developed by T. H. Holmes and R. H. Rahe in *Journal of Psychosomatic Research*, 1967, pp. 213-218, published by Pergamon Press.

Not only is each life event cited in figure 3–2 likely to be encountered by the perpetrator as a *result* of his crime, each of these events is likely to be among the stressors *precipitating* the crime. When we first introduced a unit on loss, bereavement, and grief into our work with incarcerated incest offenders, "lights" went on all over the room. Many of the perpetrators had never before realized that some experiences from their lives were still ungrieved, still insulated from the losses they experienced but never expressed. Once they understood that their feelings were predictable and normal, they could express them and let them go. Take for example the case of Pete:

> For twenty years Pete carried unexpressed grief over the life-threatening illness and eventual death of his daughter (who he had abused years before). In group that day, as we began to review Kubler-Ross's Stages of Death and Dying, he began to make connections between what he felt over his daughter's illness and death, his abusive behavior, the guilt he carried over the abuse, and with other deaths in his family. He was a large man, gruff, a man who controlled his family with unquestionable authority. He never gave himself the opportunity to grieve any of those losses. He thought he was responsible for holding everyone else together and providing shoulders for each of them to lean on. As he poured out his pain, I kept thinking of the biblical Peter: Peter the Rock, the strong one. Pete's behavior was not all selfless, he just did not know he had the right and the obligation to grieve. In group that day, Pete learned that grief is not a sign of weakness, it is a sign of health. Pete had been the one everyone else had leaned on during that stressful period of time when three family members died within a year. Pete was never aware of his own internal state until the lights came on in group that day; once they did, he had the permission he needed to begin the grieving process. As we prepared to leave the room at the end of the session, Pete said aloud "What a relief! Why didn't anyone ever tell me about this before? *Now* a lot of things make sense."

In other cases, the key to understanding the dynamics of the crime was gaining insight into the fact that the crime closely followed a life stressor: death of a parent, multiple deaths, death of the perpetrator's abuser, work-related losses, loss of relationships, and changes in balance of power within the family. It is important to work through the grief, then go back and examine the perpetrator's coping style, identify dysfunctional coping patterns, and identify and practice new, functional coping strategies that can replace the former patterns. In terms of the perpetrator's self-esteem, it is also important to explore how the loss impacted the self-concept: does the perpetrator somehow feel responsible for the loss? What role did the perpetrator actually play in the loss? Which aspects of the loss are real and which are perceived, projected, or identified? What meaning did the lost object, relationship, capability, or opportunity have for the perpetrator, family, or environment? Does the client perceive that "one of the ten pennies has been taken away" by the loss? In Pete's case, the loss was unfathomable. Not only did he lose a deeply loved daughter, he lost the opportunity to see her healed and to heal their relationship. He lost the opportunity to ask her forgiveness and for her to offer forgiveness; he lost the opportunity to be reinstated as "father," a position from which she had rightfully fired him years before. He blamed himself that she had failed to adequately care for herself when she knew the consequences. He will always wonder if she intentionally killed herself by inches because of the shame she bore for what he did.

It is hard to understand what makes people resort to the perpetration of sexual abuse, even after we have heard their histories. Perpetrators have experienced losses, as we all have, but for one reason or another they have not coped well with their losses. We have all heard it: "There's always someone who has suffered more than I have," or "I suffered because I had no shoes until I met a man who had no feet." The salient point is that those who suffer do not necessarily resort to inappropriate means of coping with those losses and injuries.

Why do some cope well and some cope poorly? Our philosophy is similar to that of Alfred Adler. Adler says that it is not so much what happens to us, as how we perceive what happens to us. He talks about "response potentiality," the means by which we respond to stress. Adler believes we respond to stressors in the ways we were taught by those who raised us. (This philosophy plugs into the W.A.R. Cycle (Figure 2–1) and the Cycle of Internalized Shame (Figure 3–1) rather nicely.) As Sid Simon says, "You get the parents you get." We cannot choose our parents. Some are abusive, some are alcoholic, some are incestuous, some do not have the foggiest idea how to parent. While we cannot be held responsible for what they do to us, we are responsible *for our response* to what happens to us. We *create* our own response; we *choose* how we will respond. As children our choices are limited because our experience is limited, but as we grow into adulthood our experience broadens and our options for response broaden as well. We no longer need to follow the dysfunctional pattern of our parents and caretakers as people who are stuck in narrow response option patterns do. As adults we are responsible for finding new, functional, constructive ways of coping. Helping to make new options available is one of the objectives of therapy. Another objective is determining how perpetrators perceive their losses. Do not assume the loss means the same thing to them as it might mean to you. We respond to losses individually. If the death of a caretaker makes an individual feel unloved or unlovable, that person *feels* that way and will react accordingly whether that is a realistic response or not! The subconscious does not know whether what we tell it is true or not, it just records our response. From that point on, similar experience will be filtered through that recorded perception. The point is simply this: when dealing with losses, be sure you listen for *the clients' percep-*

tions of their losses and work with those perceptions, helping them to take responsibility for their own responses and assisting them to create more appropriate responses.

Forgiveness

Let us begin with a model for forgiveness that we encountered when attending an experiential workshop entitled "Forgiveness: The Essential Passage to Wellness and Maturity" developed and presented by Drs. Sidney and Suzanne Simon. We strongly recommend attending this workshop that the Simons present at various times and places across the country. This material is now available in their book entitled *Forgiveness*.

Stepping through the process of forgiveness for areas of pain in your own life is an invaluable asset to helping someone else work through the forgiveness process. As a team, Sid and Suzanne Simon are extremely sensitive facilitators with a diverse and impressive combination of practical experience in psychology, education, counseling, child abuse, and with adult victim-survivors. The application of the process of forgiveness to work with perpetrators of incestuous child sexual abuse may at first seem strange, possibly because of that social desire to punish rather than to treat or forgive. But we contend that it is imperative to work toward forgiveness: perpetrator self-forgiveness, victim self-forgiveness, forgiveness between victim and perpetrator, forgiveness between other family relationships, and the perpetrator's forgiveness of the abuser in his or her own life. This does not mean therapy has to be focused on reuniting the family. In some cases that simply will not work. But forgiveness work allows individuals and relationships to heal to the point where if the parties decided to end the relationship, they can walk away from it without heaping more emotional baggage on themselves and each other. At least they understand, have explored, and have confronted the issues that were important to the building and to the disintegration of the relationship. At least they have learned something about relationships. There is always pain at the end of a relationship, but if forgiveness work has been done, the pain stands a good chance of leading to peace.

The Simons' begin by defining forgiveness as a process that culminates in the letting go of highly charged emotional responses to pain and injury in order to move on with our lives toward a place of internal peace. *It is a process* in which one engages for one's own benefit using time and energy to remove the accumulation of emotional baggage that has blocked personal growth. It is *not* absolution for the offending party, it is *not* condoning the injury one suffered, it is *not* forgetting (the memory remains, but the painful emotional response to the memory is healed), it is *not* retaliation for the injury. Forgiveness is something you do to heal yourself: it is a process of active confrontation of the injury and the injurer in order to place the pain where it rightfully belongs (rather than misdirecting that pain inward upon oneself), and then to release it to use the energy it consumed to help oneself move beyond the injury to self-constructive growth.

The Simons' identify six developmental stages in the process of forgiveness:

1. The first stage is *Denial*. Initially, most of us either deny that the injury occurred or deny that the injury had any effect on our lives. With perpetrators of incest, we see the denial working in two directions simultaneously. As we have already pointed out, most perpetrators are also victims. For many perpetrators, coming to terms with the crime they have committed provides the first opportunity they have had to come to terms with the crime they experienced. Many men in our prison group admitted to their own victimization for the very first time within the group therapy context. For many, the denial around what happened to them as children had been so strong that they had not been willing to admit it even to themselves. When the men in the group tell the detailed story of their offense, as each member is required to do within the first weeks of group therapy, we take advantage of the opportunity to explore the perpetrator's personal experience by asking a question: "Who taught you how to abuse a child in that way?" Sometimes the question is met with denial: "Who me? What do you mean "taught" me? No one taught me." Other times the question is met head on with a look of shock-inspired-truth: "My uncle Al!" Once we can begin to explore the perpetrator's experience as a victim, we can use those memories to confront the denial around the perpetrator's crime. First we use tenderness to bring the memories out from behind the denial and to explore them in an environment of caring and trust. When shifting from working with the person as victim to working with the person as perpetrator, we use a tough approach to confront the seriousness of the damage. This tough confrontation is very graphic:

> *Counselor*: Do you mean to tell me that you shoved your three-inch-diameter penis into your baby's one-inch-diameter rectum, and it didn't hurt her?
>
> *Client*: She didn't cry. She didn't say a word. If it had hurt, she would have cried.
>
> *Counselor*: How did it feel when Uncle Al did that to you? Did it hurt you?
>
> *Client*: Yeah, it hurt.
>
> *Counselor*: And did you cry, Victor? Did you cry when Uncle Al hurt you?
>
> *Client*: I gritted my teeth and held my breath. He told me once that if I cried someone would hear us and then he'd get in trouble. And if he got in trouble, my father would be awful mad at me. They was brothers, ya' know.
>
> *Counselor*: So, even though it really hurt, you didn't cry.
>
> *Client*: . . . didn't dare.
>
> *Counselor*: I wonder if your baby didn't dare cry either when you ripped her

rectum apart. (pause) What are the tears about, Victor? Are they for you or for your baby?

In applying denial to the crime he perpetrated on his child, denial is often expressed as, "I didn't hurt my child. I was just loving her!" or "She was only three years old then; that was ten years ago. She's doing fine now. It hasn't harmed her in any way." While in denial, perpetrators honestly believe what they are saying. Strange as it may seem, it is comfortable being in the consonance of denial: "I am imprisoned wrongfully. I didn't hurt anyone." The denial protects the perpetrators from the discomfort of cognitive dissonance. Therapeutically, we need to coax them out of denial in order that, by comparing their own physical and emotionally painful experience to the painful experience they forced upon their child, cognitive dissonance can force them to do something about the realistic discrepancy between "not hurting anyone" and being in prison for the crime of molestation. Until that kind of dissonance can be tapped into, perpetrators are likely to maintain their denial and thereby block progress toward their own self-forgiveness (necessary in order for them to have any degree of positive self-esteem), the self-forgiveness of the victims (necessary for their self-esteem), and the forgiveness necessary to heal family relationships in order that they can continue to grow.

2. The second stage is *Self-Blame*. Victims tend to have a hard time blaming the loved one who offended them. Developmentally, children are egocentric; everything that happens to them is interpreted in terms of "I." Children tend to internalize the blame for those childhood hurts: "It must have been because I was such a bad kid . . . was such a sexy kid . . . made him so mad . . . somehow encouraged it. . . . For healing to occur, it is of the utmost importance that the victims come to see that the blame belongs to the perpetrator. It is critical that that internalized self-concept of being flawed and thereby susceptible to (in extreme cases, even destined for) abuse by others be corrected as early as possible.

The perpetrators need to follow the same course in examining their own childhood abuse. If they believe they are "bad" and therefore deserve to both give and receive "badness" from others, they are at very high risk for reoffense. That self-concept needs to be corrected. Furthermore, perpetrators must take responsibility for their offensive behavior. We talked about the importance of perpetrators taking responsibility for the abuse earlier this chapter; we would like to refer your thoughts back to that section now. If we are to release the victim from the burden of culpability, the victimizer must assume that burden and verbally take it from the victim.

We work toward resolution of self-blame through reality orientation. When working with victims, therapy consists of reconstructing what happened and then peeling away the layers of emotional response, exploring each one as it emerges, looking for ways in which the victim internalizes blame for what occurred, and using reality therapy techniques for placing the blame appropriately.

When working with perpetrators, we do the same thing in reverse. Because the perpetrators' denial makes it easy for them to lay the blame on outside sources, they will often blame the victim or someone or something else. The therapeutic work for the perpetrators is two-fold: to accept in full the blame for what they did, while placing the blame for their own victimization with their own victimizer. The following are examples of how perpetrators blame the victim, someone, or something else rather than accepting the blame for the abuse:

- (of a three-year-old child) "She loved to sit on my lap. She knew it excited me."
- "I just got home from a long trip and my wife went to bingo. What was I supposed to do? I have needs!"
- "I was drunk. I didn't know what I was doing."

We use the same approach in dealing with the perpetrators' displacements of blame to others as we use in dealing with the victims' self-blame: reconstruct the event, dealing with the emotional effect as we go, exploring each response as it emerges, looking for ways in which the perpetrators blame someone or something else for their behavior, and using reality therapy to place the blame appropriately—on them.

- "So the internal damage your baby experienced when you rammed your erect penis into her vagina was *her* fault? . . . "Not exactly?" What do you mean "not exactly?" Whose fault was it? Who did she trust to take care of her and keep her from harm? Whose job was it to comfort and protect her? Are you telling me that your three-year-old baby *made* you abuse her?"
- "It wasn't her job to take care of your needs. *You* were supposed to take care of *her*. You were supposed to care about *her*. You had two hands and a bathroom—you could have jerked off without hurting your baby! But you didn't care about her. You cared only about yourself. It wasn't her fault you were horny. It was your fault that you used her to satisfy yourself without a thought for her welfare."
- "You were drunk? You were drunk, so it was O.K. to terrify your own child? She trusted you, you know. When she took you by the hand to the bedroom she wanted you to lay down *away from her* and go to sleep so you'd stop scaring her! But you're telling me that your six-year-old seduced you? And that it's O.K. that you not only caused her enormous physical pain, but also made her hate herself for what happened, and

hate her mother for not protecting her, and lose her father too, all because you chose (and you *chose* it Harry) to drink so much beer that you didn't care? Try it again, Harry: who is responsible?"

3. The third stage in the process of forgiveness is the *Victim* stage. The injured party moves out of the self-blame stage and begins to place the blame where it rightfully belongs: with the perpetrator. Appropriate assignment of blame to the truly responsible person can be facilitated by helping the victim to identify and explore feelings. The Simons' enumerate three different kinds of victim styles: whiny, self-indulgent, and mean. The whiny victim is stuck in self-pity: "No one knows what I've been through; don't expect anything of me; I'm limited by my experience," or "Go ahead, walk all over me; everyone else does!" The "self-indulgent" victim expresses the victimization by self-destructive behavior, by consuming alcohol, drugs, tobacco, caffeine, and/or excesses of fatty or sugary foods. This style of victim response is an attempt to fill the empty places in the victim's emotional life caused by the injury through overindulgence in something that is potentially harmful. The "mean" victim relates to the world with overt or unexpressed anger, super-criticism, sarcasm, general irritability, short temper. The anger is a manifestation of fear, hurt, humiliation, frustration, and embarrassment. Therapeutic movement through the Victim Stage is facilitated by identifying which style of relating to the world the victim uses, how the individual benefits from that style (secondary gains), and how the secondary gains can be achieved while more constructively expressing emotions.

In working with perpetrators, we again find ourselves working in both a forward and a backward orientation. In order to work toward understanding the family dynamics that enabled the perpetrator to abuse a child, we work toward an understanding of the individual dynamics that resulted from the perpetrator's own victimization. Working through the Victim Stage allows the perpetrator to transpose that victimization experience to an understanding of how the victim feels. Ultimately, the way may clear for the perpetrator to become available for confrontation by the victim and other injured parties in order to facilitate healing.

> *Counselor*: Murray, you say that you never hurt your daughters; you wanted to make sure they were protected from bad sexual experiences with boys. So you had sex with them to show them what good sex is like?
>
> *Client*: Yeah. It is my job as a father to protect my kids. You said so yourself. That's the way the world is.
>
> *Counselor*: That's part of what I said, Murray. I said it is your job as a father to take care of your kids and to keep them safe from harm. But I'd hardly call a father having sex with his twelve-year-old girl a selfless act for her

benefit. Your job was to advise and comfort her as she worked through her own experiences, not to take her search for experience away from her.

Client: (angrily) I don't know what you're talking about.

Counselor: How did you learn about sex, Murray?

Client: My brother taught me. He took me out in the barn with his friends and they all taught me. (tears run down his cheeks)

Counselor: Were you grateful to your brother and his friends for that?

Client: Hell no. I'd kill the bastards if they was here.

Counselor: And how do you suppose your daughters feel about you for doing the same thing to them?

Client: That was different. They were my kids.

Counselor: What's different?

Client: They're my kids. I'm their Dad . . . (long pause) . . . Oh my God. I did to them exactly what my brother did to me, didn't I? Oh my God. Do they hate me too? They couldn't hate me. I'm their Dad. They don't hate me . . . (tearful pause), do they?

4. The fourth stage is *Indignation*. Once the victims are able to unburden themselves from the blame and place the blame where it rightfully belongs, they move through a period of righteous indignation. Now that they understand that the offense was something done *to* them by another, they are freed to vent *outward* all the anger formerly misdirected *inward*. In a sense, this is the stage in which the cleansing action takes place. In this stage, all the anger is transformed to verbal and tearful expression as the victim rages about what was done and determines never to allow such a thing to happen again. In this stage, anger work is an effective tool for facilitating the cleansing. Clients find satisfaction and release in physical expression of anger such as beating on pillows, using floor bats, throwing pillows at wall targets, running, playing racquet sports, driving golf balls, playing basketball, or swimming. This is also a stage in which confrontation with the perpetrator may be effective. If physical expression of anger or direct confrontation with the perpetrator is not possible or is not advisable, letter writing or audiotape making can be effective substitutes.

Again, in working with perpetrators, the healing of the victim may be dependent on the willingness of the perpetrator to be confronted in a healthful manner. If the perpetrators have not worked through their own victimization, they are likely to meet their victim's anger with defensive anger or hostility, blocking the anger work necessary for the victim's healing. If the perpetrators can come to experientially understand what their victim might be feeling and also understand the necessity of expressing that indignation as a step toward letting it go, they may be able to offer themselves as a means of healing the victim's wounds. It is clear how important the anger work is to the healing of the victim; it is equally important to the healing of the perpetrator.

Frank wrote a letter to his aunt who had abused him sexually when she babysat for him just as he had abused his girlfriend's daughter while babysitting for her. He told us that he was not going to have anything to do with Linda or Kathy ever again because they had "blown him in" on the abuse charge. He read the letter he wrote to his aunt aloud to the group, then sobbing, began to tell us how he was feeling:

> *Client*: That bitch screwed up my whole life! Do you know I hadn't ever had a girlfriend? When Linda came along I thought I had it made. She was the first woman who had ever cared about me. She liked me for me, not for what she could get from me. I am so damned angry. I never realized how angry I was until I started reading what I wrote. Who the hell gave her the right to do that to me? And I couldn't tell anybody about it either. She made sure of that. Who the hell was she to ruin a kid's life like that? (long silence) Well, I've gotta admit that I feel better now. Just writing all those things and hearing myself say them feel awful good. I'd mail it to her if she was still alive. But it feels good to be able to say it out loud.
>
> *Counselor*: (After some comment and affirmation from the group, the counselor affirms the client.) Frank, I'm awfully proud of you. That was hard work, and you did it well—no holds barred. I can see in the way you look and the way you talk that you experienced some relief in writing and reading that letter.
>
> *Client*: Yeah. It felt like a hundred pounds of poison poured out of me.
>
> *Counselor*: Frank, would you like Linda and Kathy (Linda's daughter) to feel that same kind of relief? They're awfully angry at you, too. They won't even open the letters you've sent. Kathy won't let anyone mention your name. She needs to get rid of a hundred pounds of poison too.
>
> *Client*: What can I do? They won't have anything to do with me!
>
> *Counselor*: (sincerely) What can you do, Frank?
>
> *Client*: (after a long silence) My aunt's not here, but I am. Maybe someday they'll be ready to talk. (therapist encourages with nods) What do I do until then?
>
> *Counselor*: Maybe we could role play it, Frank. Would anyone be willing to help Frank? And maybe we could talk some more about how you feel about what your aunt did to you so you can begin to understand how Kathy feels.

5. Stage five is called *survivor*. There is an enormous difference between the Victim Stage and the Survivor Stage. The victim identifies with the victimization, using the victim stance as a dysfunctional means of need satisfaction; the survivor has vented anger and overcome it, beginning to invest in strengths rather than weaknesses. While the theme of the victim is, "Poor

me," the theme of the survivor is, "It was awful, but I made it! Hurray for me!" In the Survivor Stage the victims begin to trust themselves and their intuitions. They allow themselves to have a sense of humor. They can begin to help other people, trusting their own abilities to be of assistance to another and trusting others enough to know that they will not intentionally hurt them. Therapeutically, support and ego building are needed at this stage. There is always a possibility that a victim will revert to a previous stage. This new-found celebration of self is rather tenuous at first, easily shaken by experiences with minor failures, relationships with people stuck at previous stages, or scrapes with victimizing others. Just as it happens with grieving clients, holidays and anniversary dates can occasion regressions to previous stages, but ultimately, this stage is so much more comfortable a place to be that victims are usually able to reclaim the Survivor Stage with a little guidance and support.

Perpetrators go through the same process. It is in the Survivor Stage that self-esteem may be noticeably improved or acquired for the first time. (Suggested steps for enhancing self-esteem were discussed in chapter 3.) Once perpetrators can see that they have overcome their own victimization and are no longer limited by it, they begin to feel good about themselves and optimistic about their future. In this stage, work on planning for the future can be effective. Work should include constructive ways of handling stressful situations, means of relating to family and community members, ways of becoming stronger physically, emotionally, interpersonally, and economically. This is a good time to begin looking for ways of making restitution to self, victim, family, and community. It is helpful in group work to have a Survivor Stage member or two. Survivors provide provocative insights into the behavior of other group members while gaining vicarious insight into their own victimizing behavior. The contact with lower-stage members helps solidify their own healing process and inhibits regression, while enabling the perpetrators to move on to the final stage in the process of forgiveness.

Survivor Stage Client: Look, Chuck. I made it and so can you.

Client: You "made it" huh? Then how come you're still here?

Survivor Stage Client: Hell, it ain't finished. I did what I did. But I ain't ever gonna do it again. Just because somebody screwed me up, don't mean I got a right to screw somebody else up. And it don't mean you got a right either. I can't change what happened. I've been servin' my time. But I can try to do it different. And so can you. I can try to let 'em know I'm sorry for what I did. I ain't the same person I was then. Now it's my problem to prove that to everybody else. I ain't sayin' I ain't gonna' slip. That's why I'm still here. I'm tryin' to learn to do it right and to know when I'm in trouble so I can get help before somebody gets hurt. I don't want to go back to where I was, and I'm the only one who can keep that from happening. I've got to watch myself my whole life. And I'm not ready to do that yet. That's why I'm still here. I still need help.

6. The final stage is called *Integration*. Victims who reach the Integration Stage are able to see the hurtful experience as episodes in the context of their whole lives. No longer does the victimization occupy center stage. The victims are able to acknowledge that the experience was an awful segment in their lives, but that it was only a segment, not the sum and substance of their life experience. Those in the Integration Stage are free from the need to define themselves in terms of their experience as victims: they no longer need to identify with, to blame, or to hide behind. At the culmination of the Integration Stage, victims are able to let go of the emotional impact of the victimization and replace it with a sense of peace. Remembering what forgiveness is *not,* they have not forgotten their experience, but they no longer invest it with the amount of emotional energy they once did. The therapeutic work of this stage centers around self-redefinition, assessing strengths and abilities, setting new goals, and re-evaluating the experience of being victimized in a learning context.

Perpetrators need to reach the Integration Stage as much as victims do. One of the things that makes reaching this stage so difficult for the perpetrators is the fact that they have to reach beyond the identification as both victim and victimizer. If they are able to move to this point, they may, in fact, be ready to adopt an entirely new identity. The challenge will be in convincing the society that has condemned them that they can change drastically. In order for this to happen, society will first have to question whether they did the right thing in condemning the perpetrator in the first place. We all know how difficult it is to rebuild trust once betrayed. Consequently, for the perpetrator, this stage takes much longer to attain and to retain. It is here that the ongoing support of community groups following incarceration or community-based treatment is so valuable. In the case of the incarcerated offender, imagine walking out the prison gates upon release with the full confidence that you are ready to take on the world as a renewed and empowered person. That person is walking into a series of extremely stressful readjustments. Looking back at the first twenty items on the Social Readjustment Rating Scale, you can see that many of those stressors will be part of the perpetrator's experience in readjusting to civilian life. Even more of the next stressors on the list will be common occurrences: changes in responsibilities at work, son or daughter leaving home, trouble with in-laws, wife beginning or stopping work, beginning or ending school, change in living conditions, revision of personal habits, change in work hours or conditions, change in residence, change in recreation, change in church activities, change in social activities, change in sleeping habits, change in number of family get-togethers, change in eating habits, vacation or holidays. When the perpetrator walks out of prison everything changes—just as radically as when going into prison. Just because the perpetrator is returning to a more pleasant or familiar environment does not mean the change is any less stressful. Recalling that the molester molests as a response to a specific life stressor, doesn't it make sense that this point of stress should be a time of maximum support? Usually the opposite happens. The perpetrator's debt to society is stamped "paid in full" and often readjustments must be made alone.

All the forgiveness principles set forth here can be extended beyond application to the victim and the perpetrator. In fact, we maintain that if relationships between other family members (victim/mother, nonvictim/perpetrator, etc.) and with extended family members (wife's parents/perpetrator, husband's parents/perpetrator, wife/wife's parents, etc.) are to be healed, the same principles must be applied to those relationships. Likewise, there will be healing work to be done in the community. In our estimation, few of us could stand under the kind of public dissent a perpetrator would experience in a *Scarlet Letter*-type community confrontation. In this case, community education seems to be the best answer. In small groups as well as through mass communication, people can become sensitized to incest issues we have already presented in order to come to an understanding that incest is not always the result of a "bad person" viciously taking sexual advantage of a weak or a "cooperative" child. Incest is also a social failure: a failure to support and protect. Incest is a social problem in which we can intervene, a cycle we can interrupt, a family pathology that can be addressed therapeutically, and a family schism that can be healed.

Restitution

This probably sounds like a ridiculous issue when working with a perpetrator of sexual abuse. How can anyone make restitution when a child has been sexually abused? How can the child's diffused self-image, feelings of wholeness, sense of security, friendships lost over the abuse, feelings of being damaged, or innocence be restored? The problem with this school of thought is that it leads us to the conclusion that the child *is* damaged for good. Basically what we are doing is reinforcing the child's negative self-image. So where do we begin? Again, as a first step, the perpetrator must express to the victim a complete acceptance of blame for the incident, apologize sincerely, and approve of the victim's disclosure. This will enable the child to begin to see that the perpetrator is sick, not the child. It also allows the victim to hear from the once-trusted adult that his or her feelings of anger are justified. If the nonabusing parent has been blaming the child, even in little ways, it will also help that parent to see things in a more appropriate light in order to help the child. The next step the perpetrator can take is to make a serious and long-term commitment to therapy and to inform the child of this. The perpetrator can support the family emotionally by allowing them to express their bitterness and anger, without inflicting further pain by judging them for their feelings or getting angry with them. If not incarcerated, the perpetrator must also support the family financially and also pay for their therapy. Often the child and primary family members do not want to have any contact with the offender. Their need to be cut off from the perpetrator may be the highest price the perpetrator will have to pay. The perpetrator needs to understand that and continue to hope that someday healing will take place and family contact will be a mutual need.

When perpetrators approach the conclusion of the treatment program, there is usually a period of remorse in which they take full responsibility for their behavior, have learned new responses; and are now overwhelmed by a need to do something to make up for all the damage done. The need is most acute in cases in which the family is hostile to the perpetrator and will allow no contact at all. How can restitution be made if there has been a permanent cutoff? The fact that the perpetrator does not have access to the victim and the family is not an excuse from restitution. As important as restitution may be for the victim and the family, it is equally important for the perpetrator's self-forgiveness. Restitution can still be made to an unavailable or uncooperative victim. There are several options. The perpetrator might choose to be available for confrontation by another victim in order to facilitate the victim's healing, as Robert did for Christine in the example given in chapter 1. The perpetrator might choose to share the abuse experience with a group in the community in order to educate and sensitize community members to the impact of sexual crimes and the prevention of them in one of the following ways: pledge to start a community support group for perpetrators of sexual crimes; provide one-on-one support for an incarcerated offender returning to the community; allow his or her therapist to use some of the material from their sessions as case illustrations; or allow segments of therapeutic tapes to be used in professional training sessions. Most prisons disallow contact with children as a condition of parole following incarceration, so perpetrators will need guidance to ensure their choice of restitution will not set them up to fail.

Therapeutic Tools

There are many things you can do in therapy with perpetrators to overcome denial by forcing the individual to connect behavioral responses with emotional and cognitive responses. As long as there is disconnection between these three modes of operation, the denial is facilitated, preventing meaningful re-education, cognitive and behavioral restructuring, awareness of the consequences of the abuse for all affected parties, taking responsibility, and moving toward intrapersonal and interpersonal healing. As human service workers, each of us must select the best professional course of action. Refer to appropriate professionals when you are either uncomfortable with a client or feel unprepared to handle a case. Make sure you have excellent supervision and professional back-up. If you decide to take a sexual abuse case (particularly a client system including the perpetrator), select the therapeutic tools most comfortable for you and most appropriate for your style of working with people.

This section outlines six therapeutic tools we have found to be invaluable in treating perpetrators. Three involve translating thoughts and feelings into tangible, concretized language: journal writing, letter writing, and tapes. Two are behavioral in form and transform thoughts and feelings into observable behavior: role-play and empty chair. The sixth in visually sensory: video or film. There are similarities among all six. The purpose of each is to bring together behavioral, emotional, and cognitive responses; bring to awareness those responses that have been self-protectively held in abeyance from consciousness; facilitate confrontation of emotional pain; promote awareness of cognitive dissonance; and work toward understanding behavioral dynamics, making behavior change, resolving conflict, and healing members of the affected system. We have found tremendous value in assigning written and audiotape tasks to our clients. Generally speaking, perpetrators are masters of denial. There's nothing quite so powerful for exposing that denial system than written evidence of thought processes. Once those thoughts become tangible, they can be evaluated, understood, and manipulated. There is enormous therapeutic value in accessing any cognitive process and transforming it into kinesthetic processes (reliving the experience in order to reprocess, write or record, and then speak aloud about it), visual processes (seeing the words on paper or seeing images on film or video), and auditory processes (hearing yourself or another speak the words aloud). Take what you find useful and leave the rest. Modify or expand on our suggestions, and share what you find to be useful with another worker, or write it up as a journal article so we can all benefit from your creativity and experience.

Visuals (Video and Film)

One powerful tool to use in breaking denial and resistance is the visual media. Any of us who has shed a tear while watching a film in a theatre knows how emotionally powerful it can be to participate vicariously in another's experience. There are a number of powerful videos and films available to show to your groups or to individuals or families. We recently reviewed a video entitled "Why God—Why Me?," in which five survivors describe their sexual abuse experiences. After that broad-brush introduction, the video continued with another victim's story, extending throughout her life and encompassing the lives of her children. The video touches on many of the points we strive to make about victim issues and perpetrator issues. Because we have found most perpetrators to previously have been victims, we work on both sides of sexual abuse simultaneously. The victim issues often clarify the perpetrator issues. Their personal experiences open the way to breaking the denial and resistance that make getting to the perpetrator issues of shame and pain so difficult. Whether the perpetrators identify more strongly with the victim or with the perpetrator in this video, they are likely to be in a different emotional place after having experienced it. Other video recorded material is available for use. Always use materials responsibly: select them carefully, preview them, review the discussion guides, and consider your audience, their immediate response, and the long-range implications of exposure to the material before you use it. Video materials can have a powerful impact on the viewer, so especially if you are using them in an institutional setting, make sure you have adequate time for discussion, for reaction, and for gathering oneself together again before you send your audience back into their institutional environment.

Journal Writing

Writing in a journal is similar to keeping a diary. A diary is structured by being dated, space limited, and usually chronicling daily social activity—often in a positive sense. A journal is a personal record of thoughts and feelings experienced in the course of social activity and one's behavioral response to those thoughts and feelings. It is not space limited, and it may track a particular theme or themes. In working with perpetrators, the journal is used as a tool for focusing the offender's thoughts on a particular issue, then requiring cognitive and emotional exploration of that issue, culminating in a tangible product that can be exposed to evaluation and critique and later used to provide a record of therapeutic process and progress. Journal writing facilitates therapeutic carry-over between sessions, maximizes use of group or individual contact time, and provides a structure or focus for individual work on a particular issue.

Remember that people not only learn inappropriate behaviors as ways of coping (e.g., the W.A.R. Cycle), but they also learn negative patterns and ways of dealing with feelings and thoughts. By requiring perpetrators to keep a record of thoughts and feelings and the ways in which they cope with them, it is easier for the counselor to identify areas that need work. Not only are you helping the perpetrator, you are also helping yourself, as a therapeutic agent, to deal effectively with this client.

The following are excerpts from an actual journal kept by a client who we will call Carl, who sexually abused his stepchild. The first passage was written early in the therapeutic process. Look for evidence of blaming in Carl's entry:

> As I lay here I truly feel that there is no one that truly loves me. I think that there is no one left in this world that knows how to love with any meaning or depth. I still feel the pain in my heart of what [my wife] did to me and I try always to search for answers to all the hurt she directed to me. What could ever make her want to destroy so much that took us so long to build?

Initially, many perpetrators blame either their spouses or their child for putting them in the position to abuse. Confrontation and re-education of the effects of the abusive behavior on the child and family is necessary. It is essential that the perpetrator assume full responsibility for the abuse. In the excerpt you just read, Carl is blaming everyone but himself: everyone who never loved him, his wife for the pain in their relationship, and the entire world for not being capable of love. Carl was confronted with the blaming behavior repeatedly until he was able to process the fact that his wife did not sexually abuse their child, nor did the unloving people of the world. He and he alone abused her.

The next excerpt comes from Carl's journal after three weeks of therapy. This time, watch for ways Carl rationalizes:

> We [society] seem to be fearful of both giving affection and receiving it— perhaps because touching is related to old, often unconscious, sexual taboos. But demonstrations of affection are necessary for health. Dr. Harold Voth, a psychiatrist at the Menninger Foundation in Topeka, Kansas, says: "hugging lifts depression. It breathes fresh life into a tired body and makes you feel younger and more vibrant . . ."

Carl began to look for excuses other than his family to explain his abusive behavior; he still was not assuming responsibility for his behavior. At this point we focused our work on appropriate versus inappropriate touching, on appropriate ways of expressing love, and on the feelings of his stepdaughter—the victim. Emphasis was placed on use of the word "victim" and on using the stepdaughter's name when talking about the offense. The use of the word "victim" implies a victimizer, in this case, Carl. The use of the child's name personalizes the victim and calls forth all the characteristics and qualities of this particular victim, forcing the speaker to address her as a whole and unique individual. Carl rationalized that he not only needed, but was *entitled* to physical contact in order to maintain his own health. He never considered what his victim needed, wanted, or was entitled to, nor was he considering his responsibilities as a parent! Obviously, these deficits became the focus of ongoing work.

After six or eight weeks, the therapists began to maintain a glimmer of hope for Carl's healing. He began to show evidence of finally hearing and understanding the abuse and its effects on the child, the family, and himself:

> To form lasting relationships with others, we must be happy with what we and they are. We must have as deep a respect for their rights, attitudes, and feelings as we do for our own. [My wife] looked up to me to give her strength. She believed in me. In reality I am helpless without her. She has lost all respect for me and my leadership. I am not there for her to lean on. Today is Father's Day and I wonder if [my stepdaughter] is thinking of me as her father. I know that I will always think of her that way because I love her and miss her so much. I cry as I am now, when I think of all the sadness that I have contributed to her life. I believed in myself in those days.

In reality, Carl did not believe in himself at the time of the abuse. He later realized that he felt unloved and unacceptable. He also realized that his form of leadership was really power and control, not love through respect, caring, and consideration for the loved one.

> . . . as I lay here, other inmates came over and sang happy birthday to me. I was embarrassed, but it felt good inside. . . .

The men who came to sing to Carl were members of his therapy group. In the process of group work, the men learn to accept and help each other as well as to confront each other. Carl was learning to accept affirmation and affection from a variety of sources—and to understand that affection does not have to be sexualized! This passage was processed in group therapy to gene lize that lesson to all group members. After about ten weeks in therapy, Carl's journal reflected a period of depression:

> When I look into myself I see disgust and feel anger, hatred for myself, sorrow, and hurt because of what I did to my daughter and wife. I feel degraded and cheap, I feel disgustingly dirty, and wonder what makes me feel that I have the right to live after what I've caused . . . . For the almost three years I've been in prison, I think of the destruction, and alone I cry, around others I cry inwardly. My family is destroyed, torn to pieces. My wife lives with what went wrong and is filled with anger, hurt, hatred, and shame.

Counselors must be sensitive to any suicidal ideation clients may be experiencing and take the lead in talking about it with the individual and the group. Even though we work hard to help clients to increase their sensitivity, to express feelings, and to realize the effects their abusive behavior has had on the child victim, we must also help them to realize that it was their *behavior* that was unacceptable, not *them*. Carl learned to cry in front of people, starting with the members of his group. Whenever Carl would tear up, we made sure he had abundant physical and emotional support, first modeled by the facilitators, then extended by group members with a great deal of verbal support from the facilitators. This work helped to teach all group members to feel safe in expressing feelings in a manner other than anger, to recognize and reflect feelings to each other, to support each other, to accept support, and to experience appropriate nonsexual means of touch and need fulfillment. After three months of therapy, Carl wrote:

> As long as I hurt, I can find the answers more accurately. If I run, I will find the wrong way out. I learn more when I don't run from pain. Where I had the problem and didn't recognize it, and created it, is by demanding so much from [my step-daughter]. I know now that all she wanted was my love (like a father) and she thought she had to earn it. I know now that I failed her in so many ways. It almost makes me sick to have to look at my ignorance and know the love that I have in my heart. The more wrong I see, the more of a burden I feel. But I believe that this is the way I am learning what I have to learn and I'm afraid to stop because it is working for me. Hate the sin, love the sinner.

Carl was finally realizing what his stepdaughter must be feeling. He was looking at the way he controlled her and gave her privileges in exchange for her "cooperation." He was also learning that pain is a symptom of a problem that needs to be identified, examined, and addressed rather than something to be immediately (though temporarily) anesthetized with alcohol, drugs, or sex. At this point, when the reality of the repercussions of the damage done begins to impact upon the abuser, therapists need to be alert to signs of depression and suicidal ideation. This is a good time to begin to focus on restitution: "Yes, what you did was awful, but that can't be taken back now. What you can do is make changes that will ensure you will never abuse again. You can try to show your victim and your family that you take full responsibility and are genuinely sorry. Now, right now, what can you begin to do to let them know how remorseful you are?" Don't deny the responsibility you have worked so hard to help the perpetrator acknowledge; reinforce it and focus on the present and the future.

Carl continued in therapy and is still being seen on an out-patient basis. We had some dynamic sessions with his stepdaughter and wife in which he was able to acknowledge *full responsibility* for what happened, thus relieving some of the inappropriate guilt the child was feeling. Carl's wife and child were able to express to him their anger, hurt, disgust, frustration, and disappointment. Carl was able to ask for forgiveness from his wife and stepdaughter. Although the child was unable to say she forgave him right away, her healing was apparent and she quickly progressed to the point where she finally asked her mother when Carl could come home. As therapists, we were really proud of Carl when he said that he would not come home until he knew that he would never hurt them again. Eventually he did get strong enough to return home, and he has been living with his wife and stepdaughter for six months now. The family comes in every four weeks for maintenance and ongoing monitoring. Not all stories have such happy endings, but for Carl's family, the healing continues.

Letter Writing

Letter writing has been a practical, helpful, and effective tool. Used as a "homework assignment," letter writing can facilitate educating and sensitizing the perpetrator or can be a restitution tool. For instance, if you are working with a man and you are hearing that he has depersonalized his child (he is not relating to his child as an individual or as a victim), you might go over some of the consequences that his child might suffer as a result of the abuse. You can create hypothetical analogies using him as the victim, helping him to become aware of "how it feels to be betrayed and abused." After a session similar to this, you will want to give the offender the homework of writing a letter to himself, as if he was his child victim, as a means of reinforcing the sensitization issue.

The following is an illustration, using an actual homework assignment written by one of our clients:

> Dear Daddy: I don't really know why I'm writing to you. I don't really want to have anything to do with you right now. You are in jail and that is where I wanted you after what you did to me. You told me once you would stop and then you did it again. That's why I told Mommy. She told me she would make sure it would stop and she did. You can't make me do anything now, and I don't have to be afraid of you now. I don't know if you know it, but I loved you and I always wanted to make you happy. I never seemed to be able to do it though. You never seemed to pay any attention when I wanted to tell you something I did. I always had to call you over and over again. Sure, when Mommy was around you did things with us, but Joey and I knew that it was just because you wanted to keep Mommy off your back. I always wanted you to love me more. I always made up excuses for you when you didn't come home from work on time, even though I knew you were staying away on purpose. We always knew you were unhappy, but you would never tell us why. Now I don't care why you were unhappy. Was I so unimportant to you that you could use me like your stereo or your car? Was that all I was to you, a thing? Daddy, you always told us there was no such word as can't, that if we wanted to do something or be something or have something we could if we tried hard enough. You were wrong. There are some very important things I can't do anymore. I can't be alone with you anymore. I can't

be a little girl anymore. I can't have a daddy like I wanted anymore. I can't trust you. You took all of this away from me. Your exdaughter.

This letter was the *first* one written by the perpetrator, and it was re-written many times during the next few months. Another way we use letters is to have the perpetrator write a letter to the victim, the nonabusing spouse, or the family. These letters can be used as a means of making restitution when the perpetrator is incarcerated or when the child does not want to see the perpetrator. To increase the emotional impact for the perpetrator, reading the letter aloud is a very powerful experience. Here is an example of a letter written by a perpetrator to his six-year-old daughter who was his victim:

Dear Becky: I am writing you to try to let you know how sorry I am for what I made you do and what I did to you. "Sorry" isn't a very big word to say, it doesn't even begin to tell you how I feel about what happened. You were always a good girl and a good daughter to me. I hurt you and made you afraid of me. If I had realized what I was putting you through and how I was messing up your life, I wouldn't have done what I did. I want you to understand that in all that happened you didn't do anything wrong. All you ever did was love me and trust me like a daughter should trust her father. You were supposed to be able to trust your father. I was selfish and self-centered, thinking of my pleasure and what I wanted only. I never gave any thought to you or your feelings. I abused your trust and your love and then I used your body to make me happy. These are all things that no father should ever do, but I did them, and the only word I can use is "sorry." I love you, Becky. I want you to have all the happiness a girl your age is entitled to. I want to help give you that happiness. I want to do this like a good father would. I hope someday I will have your trust again. I know that for the rest of my life, I will have to prove to you that you can trust me. The first step I'm going to take is to get all the help I can in getting my thinking straightened out. I can't help you if I am messed up. I made you grow up too fast—that is never a good thing. You were my little girl and now you are angry with me. You are right to be angry with me. I haven't asked you to forgive me, I won't ask you either. How could I ask you, a victim of what I did, to forgive me when I can't even forgive myself? I pray to Jesus every day that he will help you get over what I did. You have a good mother who wants the best for you and loves you very much. I want you to understand something very important. I was the only one who did something wrong. I started it all. I used your love and your obedience and my size to do something you didn't want to do. I was wrong. Just how wrong I am only beginning to realize. You are a little person who has a life of her own too. My job as a father was to help you grow into that life with the proper values and outlook. I was supposed to love you and be proud of your accomplishments. I was supposed to teach you about many of life's harsh realities. I wasn't supposed to put you through what I did. I hope someday we can sit down and talk about this all a lot more . . . . Daddy.

Role-Play

Following the reading of such a letter, we often role-play the meeting between the child and the perpetrator. The emotional impact, not only on the perpetrator who is reading and role playing, but also on every member of the group, is overwhelming. When we attempted to role-play following the reading of the above letter, the perpetrator could not get beyond the first "sorry" without breaking down inconsolably. Despite many attempts, it was weeks before he could role-play a meeting with his daughter. Caution: During the period when the perpetrator is coming to full awareness of the implications of the abuse on the victim's life, the offender may feel self-blame and anger to the point of despondency or to feeling suicidal. To allow the full impact of the abusive behavior into the perpetrator's consciousness all at once is an enormous load to carry, especially when the individual has little support.

Once you have a sense for the involved parties, you can play the part of a significant figure in the group member's life. Usually the perpetrators are not objective enough to play the parts of people they have injured. At first they need your help to "turn the tables" and vicariously experience what another person must have felt. After a while, some members of the group may become very skilled in taking roles of victims (or of perpetrators when you are working on the perpetrator's own abuse), and both members will gain insight into the roles they play.

When you start retraining, role-play is an invaluable tool. Use it to demonstrate listening skills and to demonstrate response styles. Let the group process the experience, then switch places and let the group members play both parts and process the experience. Use role-play to stage meetings between family members to give group members opportunities to try out newly acquired skills and get suggestions and constructive criticism from peers.

We have talked about role-play in terms of group process. That is probably the most powerful application of role-play because of the vicarious experience for other group members and the amount and variety of feedback you get from a group. Role-play can also be a powerful tool in one-on-one or family therapy. Use it the same ways, making use of the individuals present. When you are working one-on-one and you want the client to experience both roles in close proximity, use the following Gestalt "empty chair" technique.

Empty Chair

Often when the perpetrator is repressing emotions and is unable to identify with the victims' pain, we use the Gestalt technique called the "empty chair." We place two chairs facing each other. The perpetrator sits in one and begins to talk to the victim, whom he imagines to be in the other chair. While waiting for the child to answer, the perpetrator moves to the other chair and provides the victim's response. Although initially this is embarrassing for some, it is a very powerful tool to aid the perpetrator in understanding the full impact of the abusive behavior on the victim.

The same technique can be used to address a variety of therapeutic issues. Any time there are divided feelings, confusion, or inner conflict, use the empty chair technique to help your clients get in touch with both sides of the issue and to work toward clarity. For example, have clients who are conflicted over how they were able to abuse their child play both sides of themselves. Have them start playing the part of the self who didn't want to abuse. Then have them move to the chair of the self who did abuse. Allow them to have a dialogue with both parts of themselves: the part that was abusive and the part that abhors the abuse. Instruct the clients' abuser side to ask the part that doesn't understand how they could have been abusive what will be lost if understanding is gained. Then have them change chairs and reply. Continue the process until the clients reach some new level of awareness. Use the same process as they role-play the victim: one part is the victim who loves the abuser, the other part is the victim who hates what the abuser did. The same technique can be used to explore other relationships or issues.

The empty chair technique is very effective in bringing to conscious awareness material that is normally too painful or anxiety-laden to acknowledge.

Tapes

We have used tapes in a variety of ways in our sessions. First, we often tape the actual therapy to illustrate specific points to the offender. For example, if the perpetrator is blaming the nonabusing spouse or someone else for causing the abuse, we will play it back to confront the perpetrator with the blaming behavior. We also may play the tape back at a later date to demonstrate to the perpetrator that forward steps are being taken.

A second way in which we use tapes, and the one we feel is the most useful, is to assign making a tape for homework. For instance, an offender was talking about his lack of compassion and sensitivity toward his family. For homework that week, he was asked to make a tape giving all the instances he could think of in which he was "cruel and heartless" (his words). He came in the following week with an entire ninety-minute tape filled, not only with "cruel episodes," but also with every emotion he experienced while recalling these situations. In the process of recalling his cruelty on tape, he cried, swore, laughed, and ended up telling us how he would like to change. Once the perpetrators start doing tapes for homework, many, many issues are brought first to awareness, then to the group. Taping their thoughts and feelings may be the first time the perpetrators have sat back and looked at their own behaviors and attitudes. They discover so many ways in which they have hurt their victims, spouses, significant others, and themselves. Therapeutic movement is usually significant after using this technique.

All of these techniques can be adapted to treat incarcerated as well as nonincarcerated perpetrators. In the New York State facility that sponsored our group, we were required to obtain advance clearance for any tape recording equipment used. In private therapy, you will need to obtain written informed consent for taping sessions and be sure the client's identity is protected. In the prison we were granted special permission to tape our sessions as long as confidentiality was adhered to. For some clients, granting permission for these tapes to be used for demonstration and training purposes can be one way in which restitution can begin to be made. Wherever you work, make sure you know what the policy says about confidentiality and recording. The tool is effective enough that you will want to advocate for policy change to allow taping if recording is limited or precluded by present policy.

Knowing When You Are Finished

Thusfar, we have suggested many tools that can be implemented to expedite the perpetrator's therapeutic movement. At what point do we make the determination that the client is ready to proceed without our help? Our position is that *perpetrators of sexual abuse need maintenance counseling for the duration of their lives.* How, then, do we determine when it is time to contract with the perpetrator for a maintenance program?

In one way or another, we are all working toward self-actualization. We all need self-examination from time to time. Once the perpetrator has been educated, sensitized, and has learned new coping skills to be used during stressful times, it is imperative that therapeutic work progress toward enabling the client to problem-solve and to use appropriate behavior when faced with a crisis. As we stated earlier, initially we will be doing a great deal of insight therapy to help perpetrators understand *why* they abused. We will explore inappropriate behaviors modeled during childhood and resulting dysfunctional adult coping patterns. We need to help the offenders recognize the old, childish patterns that they carried into their adult familial relationships and teach appropriate means of coping with stress. Chapter 1 presented Groth's Typology of Offenders and explored circumstances within the offender's primary family relationships that need to be dealt with in therapy. As human service workers, we may aid a perpetrator in finding employment, a new home, new sources of social relationships, ways to attain stability, and new ways of relating in the world to replace those that may have contributed to the dysfunctional behavior. As we track therapeutic movement through weekly sessions, journal keeping, letter writing, tapes, and interactions with others, you should be able to see the growth and to reflect that growth back to the client. Once remorse is thoroughly experienced and the offenders begin to recognize their own shortcomings, we can do less and less directive therapy and intervention, and instead facilitate self-insight and group process. What makes this work so rewarding is coming to see the capacity for insight and feelings these men and women have once they are free of their emotional baggage, and their increased capacity to give and receive constructive criticism from other group members.

Termination Checklist

We have developed a list of indicators we use when deciding whether our clients are ready to terminate treatment and move toward contracting for maintenance counseling. The clients should be:

- able to recognize their own shortcomings and problem areas;
- spontaneous with their interactions with the therapist;
- able to express a full range of emotions;
- able to reach out to and help others;
- noticeably less egocentric than when they began treatment;
- motivated in most areas of their lives;
- fully responsible for their crime and concerned with their family's healing;
- ready to assume financial responsibility for their own counseling and that of the victims;
- considering some practical and concrete means of making amends for their behavior;
- working on making new or restoring previous social connections;
- exhibiting new and functional coping behaviors;
- developing a plan for continuing counseling; and
- exhibiting a restored sense of humor consistent with their own style.

This list can be used as a guideline to help you determine when it is time to start expanding the length of time between sessions. Because each situation is unique, you will need to be able to recognize functional behavior and adjust the termination criteria to each individual.

4
Visions for the Future

Now that we have described our approach to treating perpetrators, we would like to put treatment into a more global perspective. There is a great deal of work to be done in the area of perpetrator treatment. We see treatment for the perpetrator as being one corner of a broader, more systemic focus for treating the injured parties. When sexual abuse has occurred in a family or family-like unit or system, the whole family needs treatment and support if it is to sustain itself. Treatment and support for the victim and nonvictimized family members needs to be planned and adjusted to their specific needs. Adjudication and treatment planning for the perpetrator needs to be based on the typology of the offender's behavior and focused on the therapeutic needs of the offender, the victim, and the family. Where adjudication is appropriate, the perpetrator needs to be sentenced to a correctional program that addresses his or her therapeutic needs in order to ensure that the perpetrator is not released back into the community with the same potential for offense. From this position, that a customized and comprehensive treatment program for offenders needs to be developed for each perpetrator, we have done some research into the topic. This chapter presents the information we gathered in our search and culminates with an illustration of the system of services we envision. Perhaps the work we have done will begin a thought process for you that will eventually lead to constructive changes in our present very limited, treatment approach to perpetrators of sexual offenses.

A great deal has been written about treatment approaches for victims of sexual abuse and incest, but little research has been carried out and published about treatment of perpetrators. Even more extreme is the lack of attention to the process of family reintegration once the perpetrator is returned to the community. Ours is by nature, it seems, a punitive society. The research of William Pearman, summarized in an association paper he prepared in 1983 for the Pennsylvania Sociological Society entitled "An Empirical Assessment of the Public's View of Retribution Versus Rehabilitation of Criminal Offenders," confirms the general consensus that criminals should be (1) punished, and (2) rehabilitated through occupational training and structured, disciplined submission to authority. But how does one rehabilitate a sex offender when these punishment methods fail to address the family and intrapsychic dynamics that foster the crime?

We contend that more effective means of rehabilitation need to be utilized. Work has been done on developing effective treatment methods for sex offenders; now those treatment methods need to be applied consistently. Little has been done to ease the transition back to the community and back to the primary (family) unit from which the perpetrator came. Supposedly, this is the purpose of parole supervision, but parole deals only temporarily with the parolee and only indirectly with the family. Once fully engaged in treatment, the perpetrator is a changed person going out into a world that is seen differently than before treatment. Trust relationships need to be rebuilt or built for the first time, new methods of coping and interacting need to be tried out, and, as with any new learning experience, mistakes need to be made, processed and evaluated, and corrected. The family needs to be prepared for and receptive to the newness. The reunited family will be struggling together to make something new and functional from what was once intolerable and dysfunctional. All family members need preparation and support. They all have forgiving and rebuilding to do. They all need to feel safe from harm and loss of control. They need to learn to love again. They need to have their anonymity protected. They need a fresh start with built-in safeguards from reversion to past behavior. They need to be part of a community (both family and extra-family community). They need family stability. They need to know and understand what went wrong and how to avoid recurrence. They need to understand where the responsibility for the abuse and the subsequent separation belongs, and to seek and obtain forgiveness. They need to learn to trust again—to trust each other, to trust the system that divided them, to trust themselves, and to trust others. They need to change—the most difficult thing most humans experience. They need help. They need support.

It is our contention that punishing sexual offenders is insufficient. Punishment protects potential victims for only a short period of time until the offender is released into the population again. Punishment by imprisonment does not in and of itself effect positive change in the offender's modus operandi. Punishment does not restore healthy balance to an imbalanced family. Punishment by incarceration can jeopardize the safety of an offender who is at risk of harassment and abuse at the hands of other prisoners. Punishment by incarceration is expensive. Punishment by incarceration often removes the family provider and leaves a family not only injured and in shock, but also impoverished. Punishment *does* make us, as a society, feel better. By punishing, we feel we have avenged the crime and the victim when we "put the perpetrator away." Rarely do we question what will happen when the perpetrator is returned to society. Rarely do we question what will happen to the family when it is reunited (most of the perpetrators we have worked with have families with whom they are eventually reunited). Ours is a society that claims to value the family as "the primary building block of society." Perhaps the truth is that we value the family that stands on its own and does not tax the social system. It is easy to become impatient with the family that demands constant support from society. It is time we put our policy where our social value is. It is time we made policy consistent with our reverence for the family unit. It is time we began using penal policy not only to protect innocent people from crime, but to prevent and treat dysfunction that precipitates crime, to institute opportunities for creating positive individual, group, and systemic change, to treat and planfully reunite disrupted families when reunification is possible, and to strengthen and support the family unit as it struggles to become whole and functional in the wake of sexual intrusion. If this were to be accomplished, we might accurately be able to call our prisons and reform schools "correctional facilities" rather than "penal institutions."

The Argument for Treatment

There are many arguments supporting the need for treatment for sex offenders as opposed to punishment alone. In Fay H. Knopp's work, *Retraining Adult Sex Offenders: Methods and Models*, Richard Seely, Director of the Intensive Treatment Program for Sexual Aggressives at the Minnesota Security Hospital, contends that punishment for the perpetrator without treatment functions as:

> a reinforcer of his own shame, his own blame, and his own grief, and that serves no purpose. The shame, guilt, and blame are usually the stuff from which the offense comes. You have to deal with it all the time with sex offenders. There is probably no more ashamed a group, if you can ever get to it—and if you do not get to it you can forget the treatment. That is one of the most difficult things to get to—the shame and blame model. And punishment just tends to reinforce that" (p. 16).

In the same book, Nicholas Groth says he is convinced that treatment is the best protection society can have from sexual crime:

> The crime is a symptom; the offense may be punished, but the condition must be treated. The offender must be held responsible for his behavior, but he also has to be helped to change that behavior if we want our community to be a safer one. Otherwise, we are simply recycling him back into the community at the same risk he was prior to incarceration. Incarcerating him is only a temporary solution (p. 16).

Fred Berlin, M.D., Ph.D., Co-Director of the Bisexual Psychohormonal Clinic at Johns Hopkins Hospital, points out the lack of evidence that punishment is at all constructive for (fixated) sex offenders:

> There is nothing about going to jail that makes it any easier for you to resist temptation if what you are tempted to do is have sex with little boys. There is nothing about being punished that diminishes your sexual appetite or your sexual hunger for little boys. We hear over and over again about people who have been in jail for a number of years—they are out on work release for about three months and they are back into their old offending behaviors. It is because their unconventional sex drive is still with them and it is very, very hard for many of them not to respond to that when temptation presents itself (p. 16).

In her book, *Handbook of Clinical Intervention in Child Sexual Abuse,* Suzanne Sgroi emphasizes that child victims abused by parents or parent-like figures cannot be safe in having the perpetrator return to the household unless there is family therapy that works on the issues that set the stage for the abuse in the first place: the parents' failure to protect the child, to set clear boundaries, and to use their power responsibly. Furthermore, she does not see such dysfunctional families seeking or complying with treatment without some very strong external motivation, such as a legal mandate. She sees a need for a multi-modal therapeutic approach (one-on-one therapy, group therapy, and dyad therapy in conjunction with family therapy), and she sees a need for therapy to be intensive and long-term in order to begin correcting the dysfunction. According to Sgroi, not only is it important to protect the victim from the offender, it is also important to get treatment on all family levels. We can only imagine how terrifying outside intervention would be to a family in which abuse had occurred. Again, Sgroi advocates using the external control (the legal justice system) to impose the internal control necessary to undergo and to endure the long-term therapy that is so necessary to creating change.

If change does not occur, there is a great likelihood of perpetuating an intergenerational, ongoing cycle of abuse. Groth reports that 80 to 85 percent of incarcerated sex offenders are molesters. The adult molesters, he explains, act out the crimes of which they were child victims. If it is true that the number of sexual crimes reported by a perpetrator is only a fraction of the actual number of crimes that person committed, we may be talking about a very large number of children who have been molested by a single perpetrator. If adult victims of childhood sex offenses are likely to repeatedly act out the crime perpetrated against them until someone reports them, we can expect that number of molested children to multiply factorially. The figure multiplies again when that generation of children reaches adolescence and begins to make the transition from victim to perpetrator. The idea is staggering. Now add to it evidence in the literature that adult offenders tend to offend not only against children, but against frail elderly dependants as well. How can we hope to break that cycle without treatment not only for offenders, but for all family members? If treatment for family members cannot be mandated, isn't there some way we could offer an incentive for participation—such as early release to a community-based halfway house, paid participation, or a family stipend?

Treatment for the Offender

In his article, "The Child Molester: Clinical Observations," Groth asserts that since the perpetration of sexual offenses against children is a chronic problem, the offender will need to attend to it daily for the rest of his or her life with the support of community-based services to help with what cannot be done alone. According to Groth, these services must represent a spectrum of treatment, including not only professional agencies and programs, but also, even more important, self-help groups such as Parents United, Alcoholics Anonymous, and Parents Anonymous.

We could not agree more with the need for comprehensive treatment throughout the spectrum of support services and throughout the life of the perpetrator. Groth likens the need for constant vigilance for the sex offender to the need for the alcoholic to struggle to keep his or her drinking behavior in check. Early intervention helps to keep the behavior from becoming ingrained. Once the behavior becomes ingrained, treatment must be ongoing. For this reason, Groth contends that treatment should always be a condition of probation or parole.

Therapist Skills

Larry Long and Corrine Cope conducted a replication study to determine which curative factor categories identified by clients as "helpful" in group counseling with well-educated, middle socioeconomic class outpatients in long-term therapy correlated with curative factor categories identified by offenders as "helpful" in group counseling with felony clients. Twelve male subjects in a residential treatment center for first-time felony offenders participated in an intensive offender treatment program for a period of up to eleven months. They were asked to rank the curative factor categories in order from 1 ("most helpful") to 60 ("least helpful.") The rank order of twelve curative factors distilled from the sixty curative factor categories in the felony offenders' counseling group, from 1 to 12, was: catharsis, group cohesiveness, interpersonal learning (input), interpersonal learning (output), self-understanding, existential factors, altruism, instillation of hope, guidance, family reenactment, universality, and identification. When compared with the results of Yalom's study, which the Long-Cope study replicated, the rankings were found to be similar (rho = .89) to a t-test level of significance of p<.001 (t = 6.134, df = 10) (Long & Cope, p. 393).

The results of the Long-Cope study indicate that while felony offenders may have different problems than well-educated middle socioeconomic class outpatients undergoing long-term group therapy, both groups find the same curative factors to be helpful. The issues may differ, but the approach to group work appears to be similar for both groups. Many therapists are reluctant to work with groups of felons because they believe they lack the skills and knowledge necessary to do so, and because they are uncomfortable with the nature of the behavior that brought the felon to treatment. The results of the Long-Cope study suggest that a worker who conducts group treatment for nonfelons has the skills and knowledge necessary to conduct group treatment for felons. In our opinion, anyone with experience in group work can work with groups of sex offenders.

The major difference as we see it is the worker's ability and willingness to address the issues head on and to take on a markedly more directive, controlling style than is typical of group facilitating. The worker needs to come to terms with the nature of the crimes felons are going to need to discuss in group treatment, and with the worker's own response to the nature of the crime, the perpetrators of the crime, and any direct or vicarious experience the worker has had with sex crimes. Once that has been accomplished, the worker can apply the group and individual skills already acquired to work with this population.

Chemotherapy

Groth advocates for the use of drug therapy for compulsive (fixated) sex offenders who suffer persistent sexual ideation. The ideation can be so distressing as to interfere with treatment. The drug Depo-Provera (medroxyprogesterone acetate or MPA), the only one of two different antiandrogen drugs available for prescription in the United States, can be used as a means of curbing sex drive and sexual fantasies through the suppression of production of the male hormone testosterone. In his workshops, Groth stresses that the drug is a control device, not a curative device. His position is that when sexually offensive behavior grows out of a deviant sexual appetite, we need to curb that appetite in order to control the behavior. Testosterone is what fuels the male sex drive, so it makes sense that if we can chemically reduce the testosterone level in offenders who seem to have an imbalance, we would thereby bring the sex drive under control so that related therapeutic issues can be addressed. It is hard to believe that sex offenders want to continue their offensive behavior. If they were comfortable with their behavior they would not exhibit the kinds of shame that they do. If the administration of a drug can help bring the impulses and the behavior under control, it seems wise to make responsible use of it.

At this time, in order to get the drug paid for, offenders are compelled to sue their state to get it (in states where it is available to offenders at all), unless the Department of Corrections is willing to pay for it and to supervise and monitor the administration of the drug. Groth advocated for the use of Depo-Provera for an offender in Connecticut on the basis that the Department of Corrections pays for medication to relieve other physically caused distress in inmates, why not authorize medication to relieve this distress too? Groth highlights his recommendation that Depo-Provera must never be used as a solitary form of treatment; it must be used as a behavior control tool in conjunction with other forms of treatment. So far as he knows, very few states have authorized the use of Depo-Provera for sex offenders. If investigation into the therapeutic use of the drug in treating chronic sex offenders is not currently underway, investigation should be initiated. Readers interested in advocating for authorization and therapeutic and preventative use of Depo-Provera can explore the issues, begin to raise public and professional awareness, and work toward changing regulations and laws that currently prevent its use.

In his article, "Pessimism and Optimism in Treating Sex Offenders," Dr. William Reid, Clinical Associate Professor of Psychiatry at the University of Texas Health Science Center and Medical Director at Colonial Hills Hospital, San Antonio, Texas, briefly overviews the clinical effectiveness of Depo-Provera and makes the point that "the medication must not be given in a therapeutic vacuum." He recommends a program of "individual or group psychotherapy, social skills training, cognitive restructuring, [and] attention to accompanying psychiatric problems (such as depression)" (p. 11). We could not agree more. For some offenders, careful use and monitoring of chemotherapy can control fantasies and impulses to a point at which the individual becomes available for and malleable to the kinds of treatment programs we have found to be useful. Chemotherapy alone is not, in our opinion, satisfactory intervention. When the medication is removed, the controls on the offensive behavior are likewise removed. When the controls are removed, the offensive behavior is no longer in check, and recurrence of the aberrant sexual behavior is a strong probability.

In Sgroi's *Handbook of Clinical Intervention in Child Sexual Abuse*, Groth outlines a comprehensive program of treatment for offenders that includes the same treatment components Sgroi advocates for: one-on-one, dyad, family, and group. Groth, however, sees an additional need to supplement these components with peer or self-help group experiences when families intend to work toward reunification. He also speaks to the importance of closely coordinating the offender's treatment with treatment for family members and ensuring that the offender continues in treatment following institutionalization (pp. 235, 236).

Other Developmental and Behavioral Interventions

There are a variety of treatments discussed in the literature, among them Masturbatory Reconditioning, Desensitization, Heterosocial Skills Retraining, and Arousal Satiation therapies. For a more detailed exploration, consult the work of A. Nicholas Groth as well as *Incest: A Treatment Manual for Therapy With Victims, Spouses, and Offenders,* by Adele Mayer, and *The Sexual Aggressor: Current Perspectives on Treatment,* by Joanne Greer and Irving Stuart. The latter book even includes a chapter telling you how to build and operate a behavioral laboratory for evaluation and treatment!

Treatment for Family Reunification

If we truly believe that the family is the building block of society and that every effort should be made to keep families together, what sorts of services can be provided to assist family reunification after intrafamilial sexual abuse has occurred? Our experience has been that most inmates as well as most nonincarcerated offenders do maintain supportive ties with their families during imprisonment or treatment and do attempt to reunite with their families after treatment or incarceration.

Incarcerated Offenders

For the incarcerated offender, the fact that inmates are released abruptly and sent back to a community miles from the prison environment they had adjusted to complicated reunification efforts. We propose a family-focused approach to case management rather than penalizing and then simply releasing the prisoner. Especially in cases of molestation, in which the crime is intrafamilial, we see a need for treatment for the victim, for the offender, and for nonvictimized family members. We see a need for families that wish to do so to maintain contact with the offender during the period of incarceration.

We would like to see that contact take place in the form of periodic visits designed to treat the family unit and to prepare family members for a gradual reunion. Critical to this notion of gradual reintegration is the ongoing supportive therapy of the victim and nonvictimized family members in conjunction with treatment for the perpetrator and coordinated by case management. Caution is necessary to ensure that steps toward contact and reunification proceed at a pace consistent with the victim's and family members' readiness.

The first step in the process is periodic visits to the prison (paid for where necessary by the Department of Corrections, by grant monies, or other funds), followed by professionally supervised visits to a nonprison site, such as a community halfway house. Gradually, the length of the visits and the degree of supervision could be adjusted to allow the family the greatest freedom possible. Eventually, overnight or weekend visits in a nonprison setting could be arranged, then weekend visits to a halfway house in the offender's community. During each visit, a planned program of treatment would be carried out, taking maximum advantage of the time the family has together, while allowing for gradually lengthening periods of private-time. The next step would be a period of community readjustment spent in a community-based halfway house. The system of halfway houses (similar to those established for the gradual deinstitutionalization of mental health patients from state facilities) could provide the setting for family visits early in the transition phase (when the family travels to the place of incarceration to visit with the offender) as well as during the period of gradual reunification with family and community (when the offender travels to his community-of-residence for periodic visits or for longer-term reunification treatment). The offender might thereby be released from prison before the actual release date and spend, for instance, the last six months of the assigned term in a community-based treatment center or halfway house where intensified family treatment can more easily occur. Such a program might prove to be more cost-effective than that same six months spent in prison. In terms of therapeutic benefit, the time is most assuredly more treatment-effective spent in such a program than in prison!

Postincarceration Services

In addition to transitional services, once the offender-family reunification occurs, services should be provided to link the offender to community-based programs and services designed to continue treatment throughout a lifetime struggle to maintain control. Ideally, these services would be offered by trained volunteers or professionals and assisted by former inmates as part of their therapeutic restitution. Reminding ourselves that there is always a risk of reoffense, the community must be constantly supportive in assisting the former offender to prevent recurrence. Community support services might be linked with the halfway houses to maintain contact with the former offender, to offer the reforming offender an opportunity to interact with and assist newly released former offenders, and to centralize and combine the services for all former offenders. Where reunited former offenders live in a remote rural area with limited access to services, weekend seminars for intensive individual, marital, and family treatment "boosters" at these community halfway houses could be arranged. Ongoing services for victims, spouses, and nonvictimized family members could be coordinated though the same program, thereby facilitating family-focused treatment, providing for systematic monitoring, early detection of recidivism, and immediate intervention.

Nonincarcerated Offenders

The same issues apply to perpetrators of the same type, victims, and families, regardless of whether the perpetrator is imprisoned or sentenced to a treatment facility. Most critical is that treatment be complete and comprehensive, that the perpetrator have the opportunity to learn and implement new skills and behaviors in a safe environment, to develop language, vocational, social and interpersonal skills needed to preclude predictable stressors, and to make a gradual transition back to living in community with people.

Marital Therapy

Ongoing marital therapy is a critical aspect of treatment for successful family reunification. Ronald Taylor puts it well in his article, "Marital Therapy in the Treatment of Incest":

> Marital therapy is an essential aspect in the treatment of incest. It offers the partners the opportunity to review their relationship in a healthy manner which is respectful and safe for both persons. It provides the support and nurturance to face fears and the direction in which couples can meet their needs. It addresses responsibility, anger, need, and resolution but offers no perfect solutions or magical cures. It offers a path for couples to walk away from the pain and abuse of their past toward a future of their own choosing (p. 202).

Taylor wrote specifically about incest; the same principle applies in other types of abuse as well. Marriage is a trust-based relationship. Once the trust is broken and the safety of one partner (and/or the children) is jeopardized, it is likely to take considerable time and work to reestablish that trust and build another bond.

Substance Abuse Services

Alcohol abuse programs are another important element in the treatment of abusive families, especially when family reunification is a goal. Ronald Taylor's article addresses alcohol abuse too:

> Rarely does only one form of abuse exist in a marriage and impact on family members. Whether abuse is sexual, physical, emotional—whether it involves

a substance or behavior—there are related dynamics which exist in the individual and the marriage. . . . One survey of families in which incest had taken place found a 65 percent rate of alcohol abuse by the offender, a 47 percent rate of physical abuse of the children, and a 39 percent rate of physical abuse of the wife (p. 197).

Treatment for Social and Community Reintegration and Support

Once again, Groth gets directly to the point in a chapter he wrote in Sgroi's *Handbook of Clinical Intervention in Child Sexual Abuse,* in which he points out that when we institutionalize offenders, we remove them from responsibilities of family living such as earning an income, paying the bills, participating in family decision making, dealing with parenting issues, and responding to customary social pressures. In prison, someone else manages those stressors for the perpetrator. The perpetrator's life becomes highly structured and highly predictable, there is exposure to education and treatment opportunities never before available, and there is no access to child victims. Relief from those stressors that previously facilitated the pathological behavior may allow the behavior to go underground, so to speak, awaiting resurfacing upon return to the pressures of life on the streets. Being overwhelmed by the pressures of daily living when the inmate abruptly, and without treatment, rejoins family and community living essentially sets the stage for re-emergence of the pathological behavior—for recidivism. In Groth's opinion, and in ours, we need the authority of the judicial system to ensure that the offender gets into treatment—or stays in treatment—until the offender no longer constitutes a threat to the safety of the community. According to Groth, a multidisciplinary, interagency team intervention approach is required in order to provide adequate service to this treatment population (p. 239).

Teamwork by individual therapists, group therapists, the prison or institution treatment provider, the parole or probation officer, and community service workers is essential to the provision of consistent, comprehensive, monitored service for the family reunified during treatment of sexual offense. A single case manager needs to be appointed in order to oversee the case, coordinate treatment for all family members, monitor the services being provided, ensure that treatment progresses, monitor family reunification, and coordinate and monitor lifelong treatment and support for the perpetrator and family. This case manager would most appropriately be a counseling professional affiliated with the community-based halfway house servicing the offender after release from the institution. Case management responsibility may most effectively be transferred from one appropriate worker to another as treatment progresses and geographic settings change.

Helpful community support groups outside the halfway house or prison setting, such as Sex and Love Addicts for learning ways to maintain control, Parents Anonymous for learning parenting skills and for victim and perpetrator groups, Parents United for services to the regressed offender and to each of the family members, and other local agencies, can provide various services as needed. These service providers might be invited to come into the halfway house periodically to train, educate, and advise clients, staff, and treatment professionals.

Community Education

The awareness of the pervasiveness of sexual offenses against children and the eduction of our children to teach them to protect themselves from vulnerability to sexual offense is our strongest social defense against sex crimes perpetrated against children. Bearing in mind what Groth said, that an acknowledged offense is treatable, if we as a society can acknowledge the existence and scope of sexual crimes against children in our society, we might be better able to face the problem and deal with it through comprehensive prevention and treatment planning. At present, Family Court mandates offenders to treatment during incarceration when, in reality, in most facilities no treatment programs exist. Pressure needs to be applied to the penal system to formulate treatment programs that ensure that offenders do not return to society in as bad or worse condition than they were when they entered the judicial system. Judges must become receptive to assessing and classifying sex offenders by some standardized criteria so that appropriate sentencing and treatment recommendations can be made. Professional treatment teams need to be trained and organized to provide comprehensive services to offenders and their families. Legal action must be taken to change sentencing, incarceration, treatment, parole/probation, and postrelease policy. We need to develop policies where none exist and to revamp policies where they are inadequate. Statewide planning and policy making needs to be coordinated, and those plans and policies need to be consistent and congruent with national planning and policy. Specific recommendations have been set forth in a document by E. M. Brecher, *Treatment Programs for Sex Offenders,* published as a National Institute of Law Enforcement and Criminal Justice Prescriptive Package in 1978. This document would be a good starting place for developing procedures for reviewing and improving local and state penal policy.

Individual Advocacy

Individuals are not impotent change agents. Individuals who see a need can advocate on an individual, group, or professional level. The pilot group treatment program for incest offenders in which we were involved, the only such program in New York State at the time, was initiated after a Parents Anonymous office was contacted directly by an inmate who saw a need for such a group and advocated for it on an individual level.

Direct Beneficiaries

Our entire society stands to benefit from the types of policy changes we are recommending. Economically, the cost of incarceration would be relieved by reducing the number of days of incarceration for sex crimes. Prison confinement is very expensive relative to other types of treatment (community-based services, halfway houses, etc.). Some of the costs of incarceration can be reduced or redirected toward more comprehensive and more effective "correction" of sexually aberrant behavior and family dysfunction. The freedom and safety of children would be improved due to eased reporting requirements and access to intervention services. The mental health and social adjustment of child victims would be improved as the incidence of sex offenses perpetrated against children decreases and as victims and their families are treated. Alcohol and substance abuse counseling for offenders can be expected to make society safer from other crimes related to the substance use and from the general threat posed to society by reducing the number of abusers. If families are the "primary building blocks of society," provision of the proposed services for dysfunctional families will benefit the entire society by making stronger, more stable, more self-sufficient, and more functional families. The perpetrator benefits too. We cannot believe perpetrators of sex crimes enjoy being deviant. The kinds of services proposed provide early intervention and ongoing service and support to arrest and bring deviant behavior under control so offenders can become functioning, acceptable, self-accepting, productive, and participating members of society.

Strategies for Adoption of Proposed
Policy Recommendations

First, we recommend training of professional treatment teams that can lead the way in program development and implementation and, at the same time, begin gathering data and developing measurement and evaluation tools to be used to sell the comprehensive treatment approach at policy-making levels—state penal policy, legislative policy, judicial policy—and at comparable federal policy levels as well.

Public education is the next step. An atmosphere of receptive public opinion needs to be ensured in order to attain public support for and input to the policy-making process.

Professional case advocacy can lead to some professional cause advocacy, as occurred recently when inmates of a special housing unit at Attica successfully advocated for adequate mental health treatment for residents of that unit. Such action will establish legal precedents and open doors for policy changes. Advocacy can take place on progressive levels: individual, individual and worker, class action, agency, local or community, professional, state, and national advocacy levels. Ideally, of course, it would be gratifying to see nationwide voter demand for a comprehensive treatment policy on the premise that such a policy is valuable and mutually beneficial to everyone in society. Before that day, however, we have a lot of work to do to raise public awareness about the extent of sexual abuse, the effects of sexual abuse, the need for a comprehensive system of services, the cost and ineffectiveness of much of what we are doing now, and the risks inherent in continuing as we are now.

Pilot programs such as ours will be useful in gathering information and experience to use to demonstrate the feasibility and success of such programs. Videotapes and audiotapes can be made (with proper permission, of course) to be used in training other professionals who wish to initiate similar programs. Data can be collected as a basis for evaluating the results and effectiveness of such treatment programs, measurement instruments can be developed and perfected, screening tools can be devised, cost effectiveness can be evaluated. All these things need an arena in which to be thought out and tried out. Funding seems to be available for other kinds of start-up projects and pilot programs; we suggest some of that money be used to get this groundwork done.

Program Cost and Funding

With so little work having been done on treatment of sex offenders in New York State, and with programming toward family reunification in the fledgling stages, it is difficult to project program costs, although preliminary figures may be available through State Departments of Corrections. Edward Brecher provides some thought-provoking suggestions for funding programs for institutionalized people in his work, *Treatment Programs for Sex Offenders*:

> Incarcerating an offender in a state correctional institution costs considerably more than the cost of room, board, tuition, and incidental expenses for a student at the state's university—indeed, a year in most correctional institutions costs more than a year at Harvard or Yale. Much the same is true of the cost of holding a sex offender for a year in a state mental hospital (p. 69).

Brecher notes that it costs little or nothing more to provide a sex offender with relevant treatment in a state hospital than it does to provide the irrelevant modes of treatment most state hospitals now provide; indeed, it may cost less. Though data based on experience are not available, the same may also prove true for treatment programs in medium-security and minimum-security correctional institutions. The cost of additional treatment personnel may be balanced by savings in correctional personnel not required for treatment programs that maintain their own security. The redeployment of existing funds, personnel, and resources may prove sufficient or almost sufficient in many situations.

> Where additional funds are needed, the state legislature which already supplies funding for state mental hospitals and correctional institutions is the obvious source of the additional funds as well. State legislatures are notoriously loath, of course, to supply more than minimum funding for such institutions, and very few politically potent pressure groups exist to urge more adequate appropriations. In the case of sex offender treatment programs, however, there are numerous possibilities for securing very powerful support at appropriation time (p. 69).

Brecher goes on to list concerned professionals who might go to bat for appropriate funds: judges, prosecutors, defense attorneys, psychiatrists, psychologists, social workers, community service agencies, and women's groups. He suggests organizing and mobilizing these professional groups to advocate for funds. This is likely to be a greater challenge today than it was in 1978 when Brecher wrote those suggestions. We are seeing a continuing trend toward cuts in mental health program funding. In light of that trend, it might be better to approach funding for family-focused sex abuse treatment from a penal reform perspective than from a mental health perspective.

Community-based programs need to be bolstered financially in order to allow the kinds of program expansion and development necessary to support comprehensive treatment and family reunification programming. Brecher has something to say about program costs in another sense:

> In the absence of community-based programs, many sex offenders who do not need incarceration will inevitably be incarcerated. Thus it can be argued that expenditures on community-based programs can be recouped at least in part by savings in institutional expenditures (p. 69).

Brecher recommends tapping into federal agencies and foundations as well as other private philanthropies for funding, especially for funding planning, pilot projects, evaluation, and the training of personnel. Finally, he suggests that we cannot afford not to provide services to sex offenders:

Everyone, including members of legislative appropriations committees, is concerned to curb sex offenses. Despite even the harshest laws, the vast majority of sex offenders and potential sex offenders are at present and will inevitably remain free in the community—including juvenile offenders, unconvicted offenders, offenders on probation, and those released on parole or work-release status. Community facilities constitute one bulwark against further offenses by these offenders. A community which fails to provide community-based treatment programs is thus much like a community which fails to provide police protection. This argument, which can and should be fully documented in the course of planning for treatment programs, can be cogently presented to local and state appropriating bodies by the powerful forces in the community which help prepare the plan (p. 69).

If the foregoing funding recommendations are realistic, a comprehensive family-focused treatment plan resulting from the policy recommendations we propose might not incur overwhelming costs. It might be possible to fund such a program by redirecting current financial allocations and by raising both public and private funds.

Criteria for Assessing Effectiveness and Evaluating Program Results

The ability to obtain a measure of program effectiveness is essential, not only to ensure funding and refunding, but to measure whether treatment is creating the desired behavior change. For all the effort we propose to expend to treat perpetrators, shouldn't we know whether treatment is effective? Where do we begin to work toward assessing effectiveness and evaluating treatment program results?

First, we recommend that custom-tailored pretreatment/posttreatment measurement instruments be designed in order to gather empirical data on the effectiveness of such a treatment program. An incest-specific evaluation tool must be designed and perfected to measure such variables as impulse control, tolerance for frustration, emotional stability, contact with reality, the nature of interpersonal relationships, self-awareness and self-esteem, adaptive strengths, acknowledgement of the occurrence of the offense, acknowledgement of responsibility for the offense, and ability to detect early warning signals in order to develop and implement alternate and appropriate modes of self-expression and need gratification.

Recidivism is often the measure of treatment effectiveness. Groth argues that recidivism as judged by rearrests is not a dependable measure of the effectiveness of treatment programs for the sex offender. Groth, Longo, and McFadin (1982) have shown that many more crimes are committed than for which the offenders are actually apprehended. They evaluated the results of an anonymous questionnaire administered to eighty-four rapists and fifty-four convicted child molesters between the ages of sixteen and fifty-seven. On the average, they found that offenders admitted to having committed two to five times as many sex crimes for which they were not apprehended as for which they were apprehended. Recidivism may not be the most accurate measure of treatment effectiveness, but it is one indication. In his article, "Guidelines for the Assessment and Management of the Offender" (in Burgess, Groth, Holmstrom, and Sgroi, 1978), Groth sets forth a number of criteria that need to be assessed in order to evaluate treatment effectiveness and predict future behavior, acknowledging that behavior prediction is both an art and a science. In the workshop we attended, Groth suggested that a more helpful measure of treatment effectiveness and predictability is the offender's willing and active continuation in a program of treatment following release from a penal institution. Groth finds that if an offender has come to understand the need to engage in a continuous, lifelong struggle to maintain control over deviant sexual behavior, the chances of treatment having been effective and continuing to be effective over a long period of time are increased. As Groth put it in his lecture workshop, *Child Sexual Abuse: Investigation and Assessment of Victims and Offenders* with Suzanne Sgroi in 1986, treatment helps an offender achieve self-control, staying in treatment helps retain that control—treatment is for life. Other than a willingness to commit to lifelong treatment, some indicators of effective treatment are:

- the degree to which the offender and the family have been able to function as a healthy family system;
- the degree to which the offender has been able to reintegrate with the community;
- ongoing evaluations of community-based service providers;
- the degree to which the offender is able to identify needs and to find appropriate means of need satisfaction;
- general stability (e.g., the ability to hold a job, maintain relationships with age-mates, and maintain satisfactory and appropriate sexual satisfaction); and
- follow-up test data.

Because gauging treatment effectiveness is so important to the safety and well-being of victims and potential victims, we support a method of evaluation that combines all of the above. Using these suggested criteria and others that have been found to be sound indicators of treatment effectiveness or ineffectiveness (see especially "Guidelines for the Assessment and Management of the Offender" by Groth, in *Sexual Assault of Children and Adoles-*

cents, Burgess, Groth, Holmstrom, and Sgroi, 1978), we suggest development of an evaluative instrument to be administered before treatment in combination with screening tools, during treatment as a progress indicator, at treatment termination, and periodically after treatment termination. Results can be compared and monitored for changes in response patterns that might indicate danger of regression. Such an instrument, when validity-proven and reliability-proven, would help to make the art of judging treatment effectiveness and behavior prediction a little more scientific and a little less artful. A sample research design is proposed in chapter 5, which includes pretreatment, posttreatment, and periodic follow-up measurements as one means of progressing toward objectifying of these factors. Chapter 5 also describes one data-gathering tool we found useful, the FIRO Awareness Scales.

Areas for Policy Change

We see five areas in which policy change needs to occur: Presentencing Policy, Sentencing Policy, Prison Policy, Postrelease Policy, and General Policy Recommendations.

Presentencing Policy

1. For incarcerated offenders and their families, we see the issue of protecting the victim by removing the victim from the home as a part of the presentencing process that impacts the family members from the initial point of intervention onward. The attribution of blame for the crime is an element of treatment identified as critical to the healing process, a notion encountered throughout the literature (Groth, 1978; Groth, Hobson & Gary, 1982; Groth, Longo & McFadin, 1982; Groth & Birnbaum, 1979; Knopp, 1984; Sgroi, 1982). In the *Handbook of Clinical Intervention in Child Sexual Abuse,* Sgroi proposes three choices for dealing with the immediate protection of the child from access by the offender. In order of attractiveness they are: (1) remove the offending adult from the home; (2) remove the nonoffending adult and the child(ren) until the offending adult can be removed from the home; and (3) remove the child from the home. The first option is the most attractive because it singles out the offender as the transgressor and leaves the nonoffending adult and children in the familiarity and security of their own home at a time when their world seems otherwise to be falling apart. The second option is a choice as a temporary measure until the first choice can be arranged. The third choice is unattractive because it tends to single out the victim as the transgressor and leaves the child without the support of the people needed close by in order to feel safe and secure in this period of fear and confusion.

In chapter 3 we developed the principle that the offender needs to take responsibility for the offensive behavior; it is critical to the successful treatment of both the perpetrator and the victim that the offender do this. This process is equally important to the healing of the victim. Blame must be properly placed from the initial point of intervention. The child victim is never to blame when sexual abuse occurs between a child and an adult offender. Sexual abuse is always an act in which a more powerful person overpowers a less powerful person. The child is always the victim. Policies that protect the child from the offender need to reflect that reality by making it clear from the very start who is being isolated and blamed. The offender should be removed from access to the child. Never should the child be removed from the familiarity of home and family.

We were delighted to learn that the 1988 New York State Legislative Session passed the Hoyt/Goodhue bill allowing the Family Court to issue a Temporary Order of Protection to remove the allegedly abusive parent from the home as an alternative to removing the child victim. We need to make sure all states have such legislation.

2. We maintain the perpetrator needs to be treated with dignity and respect. There are three reasons for this: (1) until convicted, the perpetrator is assumed to be innocent; (2) the perpetrator is a human being, and on that basis alone, deserves to have dignity and respect maintained; (3) treating the perpetrator with dignity and respect advances the process. The "tough and tender" approach reduces the perpetrator's defensiveness and enables the perpetrator to confess, while facilitating both the judicial and the individual healing processes of victim, family members, and perpetrator.

3. Treatment intervention needs to begin early with adolescent sex offenders to interrupt the reinforcement of associations between orgasm and deviant sexual fantasy. Irwin Drieblatt estimates that 80 percent of rapists begin with hands-off sexually intrusive behavior in adolescence. We have seen child victims in play therapy act out the role of "hunter," going about on the prowl for someone upon whom to avenge the violation of their dignity, respect, and power. Not all child victims are fortunate enough to have a therapeutic environment in which to work out these deep feelings. If we are not able to address them in childhood, we need to intervene in adolescence before the impulses are acted out overtly against less powerful others, before the child "hunter" becomes the adult perpetrator "hunter."

4. We need to explore changes in reporting requirements that presently have potential for interfering with obtaining report of the crime, confession of the perpetrator or, worse, treatment for the child victim. A change in reporting requirements could be expected to influence early intervention and treatment for offenders if the reporter and the perpetrator did not fear harsh and rigid legal retribution. In his article, "Incest in Context" (1984), Stan Taubman makes a plea for "developments that increase the likelihood of the

reporting of incest by victims or their mothers or of surrender by the of-fenders" (p. 39). Any mandated reporter working with victims and offenders knows the frustration of struggling with whether to inform clients during intake that threat of suicide, homicide, or abuse must be reported. If we tell clients up front that we must report, both victims and perpetrators may sup-press material relating to victimizing and victimization for fear of legal inter-vention and incarceration. If we do not tell them, we are negligent in provid-ing all the information needed for a client to make a choice about entering into a therapeutic relationship, we have jeopardized the trust relationship between client and worker before we have even begun, and if that trust level is broken, the worker in the best position to work therapeutically with the family will probably be rejected as having betrayed a professional trust. The system may close again, and it may become more difficult than ever to effec-tively intervene.

Incest is one type of sex offense, but the dilemma applies to other types of sex offenses as well. In Groth's opinion, the reporting requirements need to be relaxed. He described the Johns Hopkins Hospital reporting procedure: reporting of abuse is mandatory if a victim discloses the abuse, but reporting is not mandatory if a perpetrator discloses the abuse. The reprieve from re-porting perpetrator-disclosed abuse accomplishes two things, says Groth. First, relaxed reporting requirements encourage the perpetrator to confess. Crimes that are acknowledged are treatable, according to Groth; therefore, confession facilitates successful treatment. Encouraging confession is also likely to interrupt the pattern of continuing and progressive abuse and allow early intervention. The perpetrator has essentially asked for help; the agency taking the report is then obligated to provide it. Second, relaxed reporting requirements encourage hospitalization for treatment for both victim (for any injuries or diseases) and offender (for illness and/or correction of behavior). If the nonoffending parent (who may sincerely love the offender) is freed from the fear that the offending adult will be dealt with harshly and publicly, treat-ment is more likely to be sought for the child victim. Likewise, with some assurance that the offender will be treated rather than publicly humiliated, consent of the offender to treatment is more likely. Consistent with the ob-jective that treatment for the perpetrator is necessary for the protection and healing of the child victim, this approach makes a lot of sense. The objective of self-reporting should be to stop the abuse, protect the victim, and treat the perpetrator in order to prevent reoffense. We need to do more than just pun-ish the offender.

Sentencing Policy

1. Sentencing needs to be consistent with the crime committed. The first problem is that the courts rarely sentence the perpetrator for the sexual crime

actually committed. There is some speculation among the professionals we have talked with that sexual offense (particularly incest) is so abhorrent a crime that judges are reluctant to "tag" an offender with a sexual offense charge, sometimes because judges and lawyers are concerned that such a tag will put the perpetrator at risk of harassment by fellow inmates. Defense lawyers may be eager to bargain for conviction for a less heinous crime. Groth describes the "Alfred Plea," which is an option to defendants in some states. The Alfred Plea provides that, based on the existence of sufficient evidence to support a sexual abuse charge, the defendant may be given an option to work out a plea bargain with the court without necessitating that the defendant admit guilt for the sexual offense. The Alfred Plea "covers the tracks" of the offender and keeps the sex charge off criminal record, without forcing the offender to deny the commission of the sex crime to be protected legally. Once mandated to treatment, the offender would be free to confess without jeopardizing that legal position. The perpetrator could participate in treatment without the risk of having the parole board use participation in a treatment group as evidence of guilt to a crime that was denied in an effort to avoid the label and the stigma. The importance to treatment of admitting rather than denying guilt has already been discussed as a critical factor.

In New York State where we practice, many sex offenses constitute a Class D Felony, punishable by a maximum penalty of seven years of imprisonment. However, there is great latitude within that sentencing framework, if a sex offense is prosecuted at all. First, the judge can sentence the offender for another crime entirely, thereby to another mode or term of penalty. Second, the judge can, depending on his or her attitude toward sex offenders, render the minimum sentence, the maximum sentence, or something in between. Studies have shown that the offender's race and apparent socioeconomic status affect sentencing as well. On the other end of the adjudication continuum, parole boards are capricious about granting or withholding parole. Not only is sentencing a grab bag, but parole is as well.

We recommend that states look again at their judicial structure—especially at sentencing and parole policies—with careful attention to coordinating judicial policy and the treatment needs of the offender, the victim, and the family, making sure that the penalty and the treatment are conducive to correcting aberrant behavior and consistent with the nature of the offense.

This line of thought raises the issue of whether incarceration is at all appropriate for sex offenders. An elegant argument dealing with the issue is offered in *Retraining Adult Sex Offenders* by Knopp:

> Treatment specialist Robert Freeman-Longo, Director of the Sex Offender Unit at Oregon State Hospital, sees prison punishment alone not only as unproductive but as increasing the sex offenders' pathology so that they come out with worse fantasies than before their incarceration. "They come

out with more violence, they are more angry, and oftentimes their crimes escalate so that more harm is done to their victims. Prison is not a cure for this problem, and if we are going to use it as a cure, we had better make laws that say, "You are locked up for the rest of your life until you die," because, outside of a specialized treatment program for sex offenders, that is the only way to prevent these men from reoffending" (pp. 15–16).

Freeman-Longo doesn't seem to be suggesting there is a treatment-penalty dichotomy, but rather that there is a treatment-penalty continuum. Prison alone is not helpful and may even be harmful. We feel strongly that there is a need for a combination of both. Sentencing should, in our opinion, be based primarily on the typology of the offense and the offender. Judges should have latitude to sentence youthful offenders to residential or nonresidential community-based treatment consistent with the nature of the crime and of the offender. A rapist should be sentenced to a more secure facility than would be required for a molester. All need treatment intervention. The sociopathic offender needs a more secure facility, tighter controls, a longer program of treatment, and closer post-treatment monitoring than the non-sociopathic offender. Making such distinctions requires that judges become trained in typology of sexual offenders and offenses. According to Sgroi and Groth, judges tend to be less than eager to avail themselves of the training opportunities they offer. If judges choose not to add making such distinctions to their already extensive list of responsibilities, consulting professionals need to be trained and utilized by the courts for making incarceration versus treatment recommendations for the judge's consideration. Additionally, while we do have some typology guidelines, there is a need for further work to be done: our present state of expertise is not perfected by a longshot.

According to one corrections worker, New York State's Department of Corrections has studied a proposal that would designate a single facility for the incarceration and treatment of sex offenders. There are many problems inherent in housing all sex offenders in a single facility: (1) It seems unwise to label inmates or former inmates as affiliated with a "sex offender facility" as would be likely if a single facility was established. (2) At present, there are sex offenders in each of the correctional facilities in New York State—to collect them all into one facility would mean putting a great deal of distance between the offenders and any supportive family they may have in their hometown. Such distance would likely prevent continued contact between offenders and their family members. Cost becomes a factor when distance is considered. The cost of state-funded transportation and housing for family members while visiting a penal institution would be economically prohibitive. Many families of offenders struggle to make a living while the traditional breadwinner is incarcerated; they would not be able to afford the added cost of visits at their own expense. Because we favor family treatment, the cost and distance factors would make a comprehensive family treatment plan un-feasible. (3) Services to families cannot be mandated. The family members have committed no crime, so they are not obligated to obey the will of the court. Family participation in a visitation or family reintegration program of the type we propose would have to be voluntary. Again, we can expect to encounter complications of time, distance, cost, and willingness. While size-able costs would be incurred for professional services for such a program, the cost to society is greater when services are not adequately provided. Recidivism takes on a new perspective when one wonders whether one's own child will be the next victim of an untreated offender.

2. We need a standardized typology of sex offenders that can be used to assure: (a) uniformity in typing, sentencing, and treatment planning for victims, family members, and perpetrators; (b) accurate assessment of risk factors to enable prediction of the degree and direction of risk proposed by a perpetrator and to allow the design and implementation of better prevention and early intervention programs and techniques; (c) work toward judicial and legislative reform; (d) better, more effective casework; (e) a starting place rather than pronouncing all sex offenders intractable and untreatable, thereby arresting our efforts to interrupt the bi-directional, intergenerational cycle of abuse.

Groth's typology is one of several that have been or are being developed. Knight, Schneider, and Rosenberg have presented others in their work, "Classification of Sexual Offenders: Perspectives, Methods, and Validation" found in *Rape and Sexual Assault: A Research Handbook.* Fay Knopp (1984) notes that Robert Prentky, Director of Research at the Massachusetts Treatment Center in Bridgewater, is, along with his colleagues, in the final stages of developing and validating a sex offender classification system based on ex-tensive clinical observation of 460 offenders and on an empirical base com-prised of 1,400 variables per offender. The most recent word on this work is that much of the research has been completed; initial information about the study can be obtained upon request from M.T.C. at Bridgewater. Work on typologies of offenders needs to be continued and, ultimately, standardized in order to develop better treatment approaches, to identify any particular social or psychological conditions that seem to predispose an offender to commit sex offenses in order that early intervention and prevention services can be developed and utilized, and to improve judicial decision making and legislative reform to better address reporting, casework, sentencing and ap-peal, disposition, assessment, treatment and treatment termination, release, parole or probation, postrelease services, and recidivism of offenders.

3. Treatment should be the objective of sentencing, therefore, sentencing should include careful consideration of the alternatives: incarceration, community-based treatment, or some combination of both. Some sex of-fenders are more dangerous to the general population than others. As elab-

orated upon in chapter 2, molesters tend to be nonviolent as opposed to rapists who are violent in the commitment of the sex crime. Regressed molesters tend to exert less pressure or force in engaging a victim than do fixated molesters. Sex offenders are sometimes at risk of harm from fellow prisoners during incarceration, sometimes due to the sexual or violent nature of their crime, sometimes due to the physical and personality characteristics that are common to molesters. Incarceration is an expensive and perhaps excessive means of supervising regressed offenders. Additionally, the social structure of prison is not the same as the social structure of the community or of the family. For regressed molesters, treatment may be more effective and more realistically tested out in an atmosphere that more closely approximates the social structure to which they will ultimately be returned. For some types of offenders, there are more constructive environments for treatment than the prison environment. For some molesters, a nonpunitive treatment environment can be most effective when used in treatment planning in conjunction with incarceration. Prison is a closed authoritative system not unlike the "family fortress" that often typifies the sexually abusive family structure. Perpetrators need exposure to a more "real-world" environment in which they can learn to function as responsible members of social systems.

Before we began research and treatment with incarcerated sex offenders, we held a humanistic belief that prison confinement was an inappropriate and ineffective form of public retribution compared with a program of offense-specific treatment. That opinion has undergone some modification as we have explored the research literature and worked with perpetrators. One of the points of departure was attendance at an intensive workshop mentioned earlier, presented by Sgroi and Groth. The workshop confirmed our own acquired sense of the value of adjudication, probation, imprisonment, and parole as methods of imposing needed controls on offenders who are unable to impose their own controls. Sgroi contends that consideration must be given to the type of crime perpetrated. She advocates for treatment in a secure setting for perpetrators of rape, believing that rapists need to learn to deal· with people without violence before they can function within a community. She contends that rapists need the external controls imposed by prison, parole, and probation before they can function in society: the community does not have enough external controls to teach rapists self-control until they have experienced the behavior-modification environment of the inside of the penal system. After working with perpetrators both in and out of prison, we agree.

We agree that rapists and most fixated offenders need to experience the prison environment, but not all perpetrators need the prison environment. In Sgroi's *Handbook of Clinical Intervention in Child Sexual Abuse,* Groth provides several criteria for recommending community-based treatment for perpetrators of molestation: (1) the offenders must accept at least a modicum of responsibility for their actions and be at least somewhat remorseful; (2) the offenders must be nonviolent; (3) the offense must be of the regressed type rather than the fixated type; (4) the offenders must not be chronic law-breakers (must have no criminal record aside from the instant offense); (5) the offenders must be free of serious psychopathology, disabling conditions, or active alcoholism or substance abuse and must have adequate social and occupational skills which enable them to be productive members of society; and (6) the offenders must have adequate access to and willingness to use community mental health services, employment opportunities, and other social support services that can serve to help them eliminate significant stressors and that can monitor their behavior.

Groth's criteria for community-based treatment for molesters compliments Sgroi's argument for incarceration of rapists. Based on our own experience and confirmed by the combination of Groth's and Sgroi's work, we suggest that policy for adjudication and sentencing of perpetrators of sex offenses should reflect both the nature of the crime committed and the relative danger to the free population caused by the degree of security or freedom of the offender during the period of penalty and treatment.

4. As elaborated previously, we recommend that professionals (lawyers, judges, counselors, law guardians, etc.) involved in the adjudication process be educated and trained to make case-by-case determinations about whether treatment should occur concurrently with incarceration, in place of it, or in conjunction with it. At the very least, these professionals need to listen with an educated ear to the recommendations of assessment and treatment specialists in positions to make such recommendations.

5. We need to develop an array of treatment facilities and techniques designed to treat the whole spectrum of sexual offenses and victims. We need a variety of treatment settings, levels of care, and support services.

6. We need to sentence perpetrators to treatment. If correctional facilities are not equipped to treat perpetrators, they should be sentenced to a treatment program with an uncompromising legal mandate to comply. Failure to comply should carry a penalty of incarceration until the perpetrator is able to fully engage in an appropriate level of treatment.

7. We need to sentence adolescent sex offenders to treatment. According to Groth, most of the offenders he worked with at a Connecticut correctional institution committed their first sex offense at age sixteen. In *Retraining Adult Sex Offenders: Methods and Models* (1984), Knopp says:

> Though differences exist among treatment providers as to their underlying theories or the efficacy of one particular treatment approach over another, there is common agreement that a substantial number of sex offenders begin

their habitual sexually assaultive patterns as adolescents and that the earlier the intervention the greater the potential for disrupting these patterns (p. xiii).

Clearly, in order to intervene in the abusive process early enough to protect the maximum number of child victims, to avoid repeated time-consuming and expensive adjudication and incarceration, and to treat the offender before the sexually aberrant behavior becomes ingrained, it would make sense to treat youthful offenders rather than simply punish them.

In Knopp's *Retraining Adult Sex Offenders: Methods and Models*, Gene G. Able, M.D., former Director of the Sexual Behavior Clinic of the New York State Psychiatric Institute in New York City, sheds some light on the progression from youthful sexually aberrant behavior to adult sexually criminal behavior:

> Many adolescents start to use fantasies . . . masturbate, and have orgasm. That is the key for them developing a persistent deviant arousal. That is a very critical issue. When you see these kids by the time they have committed a few crimes, they have started to use and associate those deviant fantasies with orgasm. That has to be disrupted early. . . . This behavior is incorporated into their sexual fantasies and into their sexual lives. By the time we see some adult child molesters, they may only be able to have intercourse with an adult female as long as they fantasize about young children. In other words, it has become chronic. When the problem becomes chronic, it takes on a life in and of itself because now a few activities are used hundreds and thousands of times as they relive those highly erotic experiences. When there is a pairing or association between those fantasies and orgasm, that welding together makes the problem chronic and much more difficult to deal with. Trying to unglue that by the time they are 30 or 40 years old is a major undertaking. It can be done, but if you had your druthers, you wouldn't. It would be better to approach them when they are kids (p. 11).

In the same book, Irwin Dreiblatt, Ph.D., of Pacific Psychological Services in Seattle, Washington, estimates that "80 percent of persons who rape may start their assaultive patterns with "hands-off" sexual behaviors (exhibitionism, voyeurism, obscene phone calls, frottage, and so forth)" (Knopp, p. 12).

In light of these findings, we assert that early intervention with youthful offenders of "hands-off" offenses such as those Dreiblatt describes might enable early intervention and treatment that might prevent more serious "hands-on" offenses. Youthful or first offenders should be mandated to treatment in community-based residential or nonresidential treatment facilities, the choice to be determined by the nature and severity of that first offense.

Treatment needs to focus on disrupting a developing pattern of aberrant sexual behavior.

Prison Policy

1. We need to explore the use of antiandrogen medication for hormonal control of sex drive and sexual fantasies in male sex offenders to supplement other forms of crime-specific treatment. Discussion of use of such chemicals appeared earlier in this chapter in the Chemotherapy section.

2. Parole boards need to be educated about the dynamics of sexual abuse and treatment and need to carefully evaluate parole eligibility in terms of progress in treatment and danger to the community if the inmate is released on parole. Parole boards also need to consider the professional judgment and recommendations of treatment providers as part of evaluating an inmate's parole eligibility. Our experience has been that not only were treatment providers not consulted as part of the eligibility evaluation, but any documentation that inmates requested for their files may or may not be reviewed prior to the hearing, at the discrimination of the board.

3. Upon release, we would like to see a mandatory service connection with a community-of-residence service provider who can provide continued treatment for the parolee. Because many former inmates have trouble finding and keeping jobs after they have been in prison, a funding source will need to be found to pay for this continuing service until the inmate becomes stabilized as a self-supporting worker. Whatever the cost, it is likely to be considerably less than the cost of continued risk to society if the perpetrator is not adequately treated and monitored.

4. There is a need for case coordination with victims and nonvictimized family members, overseen by a single case manager who can see that the needs of all involved individuals are addressed, coordinated, and communicated among all involved treatment providers. There will be notable problems in enlisting the cooperation of nonmandated family members, obtaining funding, and in the logistics of case coordination; solutions will need to be found.

Postrelease Policy

1. We see a need for mandatory, lifelong treatment and treatment monitoring for offenders by community-of-residence treatment providers, or community-based treatment facilities that provide treatment during or in place of incarceration.

2. We envision a link with community-of-residence self-help groups, such as Parents Anonymous, Parents United, and Alcoholics Anonymous, as a critical link in preserving the treatment effect and in preventing recidivism.

3. Continuing care for victims and nonvictimized family members should be guaranteed during the family reintegration process. This is a critical time for the victim and family members who are investing renewed trust in the perpetrator, and they must have all the support they need.

General Policy Recommendations

1. We need to continue and intensify our research and data gathering efforts. Therapeutic programs need to be designed to include pretreatment and posttreatment measures of behavior and attitudes so that we can determine when treatment is correlated with change and nonrecidivism. We need to know whether what we are doing to treat perpetrators is effective, under what circumstances, and for how long. We need to find ways to get follow-up measurements after perpetrators are released from prison or terminated from treatment programs. We need to find more accurate ways to monitor recidivism and collect useful data about recidivists. We need to develop better pretreatment and posttreatment instruments geared for the perpetrator population, many of whom are functionally illiterate, culturally disparate, or non-English speaking. Instruments such as the Minnesota Multiphasic Personality Inventory (MMPI), the Multiphasic Sex Inventory, and the Fundamental Interpersonal Relationship Orientation (FIRO) Awareness Scales are useful, but surely we can custom design instruments that will yield even more of the kinds of information we need. We need to develop research questions that can be empirically tested to yield useful data.

2. We need to educate the educators and the treatment providers of the future. We mentioned the need for public education, but we did not mention the need to educate the educators. Groth, Hobson, and Gary, in their article "The Child Molester: Clinical Observations" (1982), point out that while identification and treatment of offenders is a critical factor in fighting sexual molestation of children, few graduate programs are training clinicians to become sensitized to the need for perpetrator assessment, treatment, and services. Without trained service providers, offenders tend to be recycled back into the community without the kinds of services needed to reduce the risk of recidivism. They postulate that the adequacy of treatment and support services requires an interagency and multidisciplinary team approach to open communication and cooperation across the variety of interveners who play a role in the management of the sex offender (therapists, courts, parole or probation officers, social workers, etc.).

3. There is a need for communication and cooperation among the service providers who extend services to the spouse or significant other, the victim, the nonvictimized family members, and the perpetrator. We envision the case manager as the individual who coordinates services, oversees progress, and

makes system-wide treatment recommendations based on the abilities, progress, and readiness of all parties.

Conclusions

A great deal of work remains to be done in order to begin to attack the social problem of sexual abuse at its root causes and to treat it systemically with special emphasis on family treatment and reintegration. In preparing this chapter, we have attempted to explore some of the current thinking and literature on this topic and to formulate some policy recommendations designed to facilitate constructive change.

Sexual crimes perpetrated against children are reaching staggering proportions in our society. It is time we stopped slapping bandages on these deep physical, emotional, and family wounds and started (wherever appropriate) treating the disorder in a comprehensive, family-oriented manner that reflects our social claim of valuing the family as an essential building block of our society. If we are to protect victims we need to treat perpetrators rather than just punish them. If we are to preserve the family, we must treat family dysfunctions systemically at both the family level and the community level. It is time we put our social policy efforts where our social value is purported to be.

We conclude this chapter with an illustration of the coordinated system of services we believe needs to be operational in order to provide the intervention necessary to address the whole system once a sex offense has occurred and to attempt to intervene to prevent reoccurrence. Figure 4–1 is a summary of the more detailed Comprehensive System of Services presented in figure 4–2.

This whole chapter has been dedicated to the need for policy changes that would provide a system of services to ensure adequate treatment for the offender and to provide for the reunification of the family, but we have yet to describe the process of developing a treatment program for the incarcerated offender. At this point we will shift focus and describe the pilot program one author designed and initiated for the treatment of incest offenders in one of upstate New York's correctional facilities.

FIGURE 4-1

**Outline of Coordinated System
of Services for
Sex Offender Treatment**

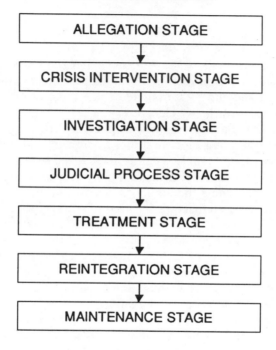

ALLEGATION STAGE

CRISIS INTERVENTION STAGE

INVESTIGATION STAGE

JUDICIAL PROCESS STAGE

TREATMENT STAGE

REINTEGRATION STAGE

MAINTENANCE STAGE

FIGURE 4-2

Coordinated System of Services for Sex Offender Treatment

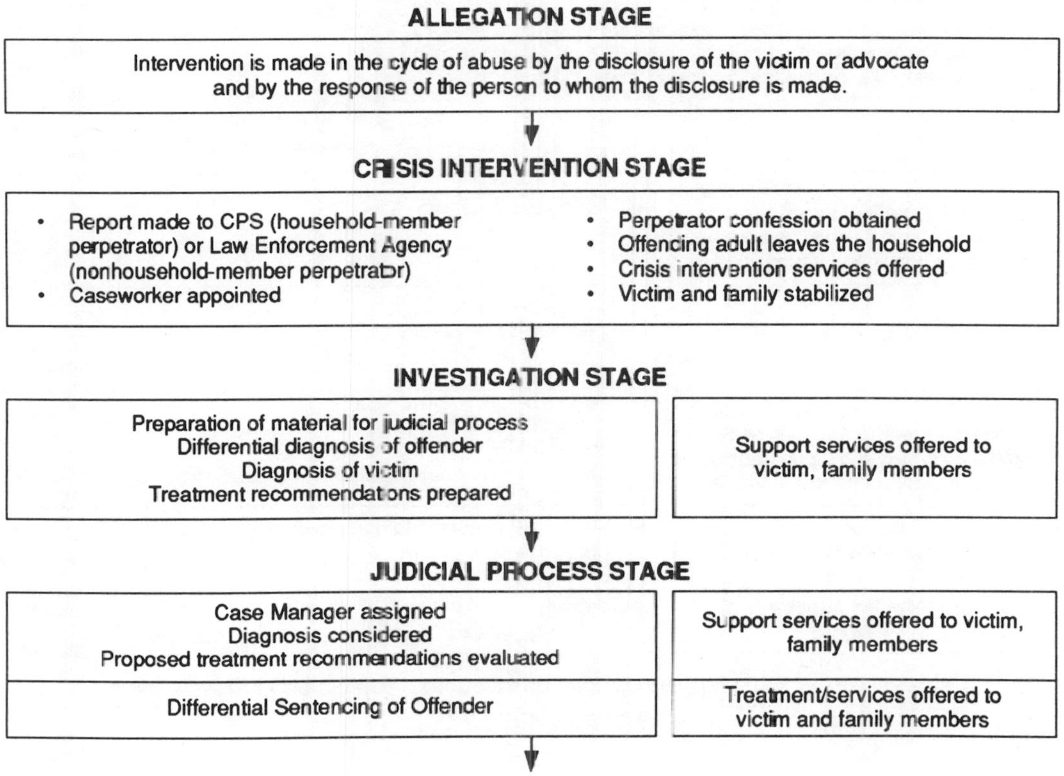

ALLEGATION STAGE

Intervention is made in the cycle of abuse by the disclosure of the victim or advocate and by the response of the person to whom the disclosure is made.

CRISIS INTERVENTION STAGE

- Report made to CPS (household-member perpetrator) or Law Enforcement Agency (nonhousehold-member perpetrator)
- Caseworker appointed

- Perpetrator confession obtained
- Offending adult leaves the household
- Crisis intervention services offered
- Victim and family stabilized

INVESTIGATION STAGE

Preparation of material for judicial process
Differential diagnosis of offender
Diagnosis of victim
Treatment recommendations prepared

Support services offered to victim, family members

JUDICIAL PROCESS STAGE

Case Manager assigned
Diagnosis considered
Proposed treatment recommendations evaluated

Differential Sentencing of Offender

Support services offered to victim, family members

Treatment/services offered to victim and family members

Figure 4–2. Continued

TREATMENT STAGE

Case Manager coordinates treatment/services among ALL providers and clients

	RAPIST			MOLESTER		VICTIM AND FAMILY MEMBERS
	Sadistic	Power	Anger	Fixated	Regressed	
Length of Sentence / **Length of Treatment/Services**	← Long-term ─ ─ ─ ─ ─ ─ ─ ─ ─ ─ ─ ─ ─ ─ Shorter-term →					As needed over lifetime
	← ─ ─ ─ ─ ─ Lifelong Treatment and Monitoring ─ ─ ─ →					
Treatment Program	← Psychiatric/Behavioral/Developmental →			← ─ ─ Psychosexual/Psycho-social Retraining ─ ─ →		Recommendations for treatment program and mode based on needs assessment (individual – group – support services).
Treatment Mode	← Individual, supplemented by group ─ ─ →			← Group, supplemented by individual ─ ─ →		
Treatment Facility	← ─ ─ ─ Security Intensive ─ ─ ─ →			← ─ ─ Treatment Intensive →		By decision of victim, family members, and Case Manager. Should provide range of services to ALL affected parties.
Course of treatment toward reunification with primary systems	← Minimal. Supervised meetings only at initiation of victim(s), family members, and Case Manager					As treatment progresses, and as the judgment of the Case Manager deems constructive, periodic supervised therapeutic session with spouse, progressing gradually to less-restrictive supervision and setting, progressing gradually toward family session, progressing gradually toward supervised perpetrator/victim therapy sessions at the discretion of victim, therapist(s), and Case Manager.

Figure 4–2. Continued

REINTEGRATION STAGE

- - - Emphasis on Community Reintegration
overseen by Case Manager

- - - Emphasis on Family and Community Reintegration
coordinated and supervised by Case Manager

Release to RESIDENTIAL TREATMENT facility in community of residence for continued work on sex offender issues in conjunction with psychosocial retraining, vocational/job preparation, substance use treatment, family reintegration, connections with community-based self-help and support groups.

Input to and co-therapy with community-of-residence treatment staff. Co-therapy with offender.

OUTPATIENT TREATMENT conditional upon successful completion of residential program; evidence of minimal threat to community, victim(s), and family; continuation with self-help and supportive services (P.A., A.A., Parents United, Aftercare, etc.); continuation of therapeutic work with community of residence treatment provider on continuously less-restrictive basis (weekend "boosters," Aftercare, ongoing marriage/family therapy); and stable employment.

Input to and co-therapy with outpatient treatment program providing both individual and family services as assessed needed by Case Manager.

- - - Therapeutic Restitution completed - - -

- - - Family Reunited - - -

MAINTENANCE STAGE

- - - Lifelong treatment and monitoring services to offender, victim, family, - - -
coordinated and supervised by Case Manager.

5
A Group Treatment Model for Incarcerated Perpetrators

U nfortunately, incarceration alone does not stop the sexual abuse of children. Demands by politically active social lobbies, including the feminist movement, have increased pressure to make therapy available to incarcerated sex offenders. This chapter describes a group approach to therapy with incarcerated perpetrators that was developed as a response to the need highlighted by these social pressures.

Group Model

The model for initiating group treatment for incarcerated perpetrators of incest and incest-like offenses emerged from our research and our grass roots approach to the problem. The model contains seven components organized according to the significance of each aspect of the group process:

1. Identification and background of potential group members.
2. Individual interview of group candidates.
3. Initial group meeting.
4. Development of personal responsibility.
5. Working through issues emerging from assuming personal responsibility.
6. Re-education and sensitization.
7. Termination.

Identification and Background of Potential Group Members

Routine groundwork is essential in preparing for any group. In preparing for this group, the professional counseling staff at the prison was canvassed to identify suitable group candidates presently on their case loads. Group candidates were proposed based on case histories of sex offenses. Group facilitators then reviewed those case histories and selected candidates who appeared to be nonviolent offenders (molesters, as opposed to rapists). Inmates were recruited through their corrections counselors and were then invited for a screening interview with the group facilitators. There was no penalty for failing to participate. No assurance was given that participation would benefit the inmate in any way. Inmates were encouraged to consider group membership for their personal benefit, rather than for any institutional benefit.

During this process, our literature-affirmed speculation that incest becomes a carefully guarded "family secret" in incestuous families became experientially confirmed. Each interviewee expressed extreme concern about anonymity. In several cases the opportunity for counseling was rejected only because it would threaten the facade these perpetrators had constructed to hide the nature of their offense. Historically, in the prison where our groups lived and met, sex offenders have been vulnerable to harassment by other inmates for the sexual nature of their crime. We mentioned earlier that the corrections counselor we worked with does not believe sex offenders are at any unique risk because of the nature of their crime. In his opinion, if there is risk it is due to the physical characteristics typical of the average regressed molester (on the average, regressed offenders tend to be smaller-framed individuals) or the personality characteristics (regressed offenders, on the average, tend to be quiet, nonaggressive, nonassertive individuals who lack the social skills that would make them appealing in peer relationships). Rapists are also unpopular in prison populations because of their physical and personality characteristics (on the average, rapists tend to be physically larger and more powerful, more anger-motivated, more aggressive, and less socially adept). The concern about anonymity for the regressed offender seems consistent with the "family secret" (the history of intrafamilial sexual abuse is kept secret from the prison world as well as from the outside world) and with the cycle of internalized shame (the offender feels shame, is adjudicated for committing a shameful act, believes himself or herself to be a shameful person, and defends against further shame by maintaining anonymity and a low profile in prison). The risk of identifying with a group of sex offenders may indicate dual fears: genuine fear of physical harm from other inmates compounded by fear of risking more shame, judgment, and punishment should they be identified as sex offenders.

Following from our experience, expect some reluctance to participate in sex-offense-specific therapy. You may want to cover your tracks in order to reassure your candidates. One of the ways we helped to overcome the fear of exposure was to call ourselves something else. From the outset of interviews, we identified ourselves to other inmates as a group sponsored by Parents Anonymous that taught parenting skills to inmates; *part* of who we were as a group. We traded off protecting the family secret for protecting the inmate.

That decision was made with the foreknowledge that the family secret would be exposed and explored within the confines of the therapeutic group. In a very real sense, sex offenders join AIDS victims as society's modern-day outcasts. Once the disorder becomes public knowledge, these people are branded as deviant, dangerous, and not deserving of the full benefits of membership in society. It's awful and it's wrong, but that's the way it is for the present. In the future, we may be able to produce evidence that treatment for sex offenders renders them free from harming others, free from socially deviant behavior. In the meantime, the fear of social disconnection is founded in experience.

Another measure taken to avoid sex offender identification for the group was to meet during regularly scheduled program hours, within the area of the prison where other routine programs meet; to do otherwise would arouse the curiosity of other inmates and encourage investigation. Prisons are institutional bastions of regimentation and conformity in which it is very hard to keep anything hidden. Efforts to detract attention seem only to attract it. For those of you considering starting groups for incarcerated offenders, we recommend you work with the system, not against it. For those of you working in community settings, you will undoubtedly find similar dynamics operating. Set these groups up in the same way you would set up any other group with the obvious exceptions of treatment-specific issues.

Individual Interview of Group Candidates

Before meeting as a group, it is necessary to interview the candidates and determine whether they are appropriate for the group. Questionnaires were prepared, pretested, and revised to meet the needs of making such a determination.

Sample questions from the instrument we use are provided to give you an idea of how we got started. You may want to modify it for your own use. The questionnaire was initially filled out by the prospective group member, then used as a guideline for the face-to-face interview that followed:

1. What was the nature of your crime?
2. Describe your victim.
3. Were there any previous victims?
4. Whose responsibility was the crime?
5. What was your family situation at the time of the crime?
6. Describe yourself today:
   What are your likes and dislikes?
   Who are you?

What do you feel you can offer society once released?
How would you like to be viewed by others?

7. Are you willing to share in a group dealing specifically with sexual abuse? Do you feel you can be honest in dealing with this crime within a group setting?

8. What are your expectations of a group that deals with this type of offense?

9. What would you like to change if accepted into a group?

10. Do you deserve to be forgiven?

Responses to these questions supplied valuable information to the counselors:

Question 1, regarding the nature of the crime, gave us a fairly good idea of whether the abuser is ready to deal with and take responsibility for the crime. Confrontation and the stripping away of rationalizations began during this first contact with the offender. We found that an inmate's willingness to discuss the crime did not necessarily make the inmate a good candidate for the group. Other factors needed to be considered as well. On the other hand, if the inmate denied committing the crime, it became necessary to probe deeper to determine whether it would be detrimental to other group members' growth to allow that inmate into the group. It is important that, for incarcerated offenders, you have the offense record in front of you during the interview in order to corroborate or refute what the inmate is telling you. If your candidates are not incarcerated, make sure you have gathered all available information from cooperating lawyers, probation officers, physicians, caseworkers, police, or courts for the same purpose of checking the accuracy of the client's story.

The "instant offense" refers to the offense for which the inmate was brought to the attention of the law enforcement authorities. Some were ready to talk about their crime and to seek help:

> "I went into my daughter's room late at night. I was lonely and I just wanted to sleep beside someone warm. I laid down beside her and she cuddled right up to me. I must have gone to sleep, because the next thing I knew she was crying and saying "Daddy, you're hurting me." My penis was in her. I don't know how it happened. I would never hurt my daughter. I want to find out why I did that in my sleep."

Others, like Al, needed the structure and supportive community of the group in order to expose their guilt and talk openly about their crimes:

Al, a sixty-year-old white man, was convicted of incestuous relations with his thirteen-year-old daughter. When interviewed, he denied his guilt, but said he would like to be part of the group. After sitting through two hours of the group, it was his turn to tell the nature of his crime. He told the group about an incestuous relationship with his daughter who was now twenty-nine years old—a crime committed sixteen years previously. He cried throughout the disclosures and did not stop until all the details had been revealed.

Questions 2 and 3 ask the perpetrator to describe the victim(s), and prompted very emotional responses from some perpetrators. They appeared to have repressed thoughts of their victim's experience: naming and describing the child victim became an overwhelming and emotional task. We find the experience to be extremely helpful for the counselor in understanding the abuser's level of insight. It also gets therapy off to a good start by defining the degree of specificity that will be part of group work, and the degree to which confrontation with reality can be expected. After the initial interview, any illusions about the seriousness of the work to be done by the group is dispelled; the perpetrators come to the first meeting prepared to work and work hard.

Questions 4 and 5. Initially, when asked about their family situation at the time of the offense, many perpetrators blamed their spouses for the crime they committed. Although it served as a defense or coping mechanism, the inmate was not allowed to play the "blame game" either during the selection interview or later in the group process. Several weeks into the group process, most of the inmates admitted they were responsible for the crime, *but* they needed to be loved and cared for by someone; the victim was seen as someone who loved them. From that point on, therapeutic work focused on dispensing with the "but." The perpetrators are relentlessly pushed to examine their behavior as a *choice* rather than as something they did in passive response to someone or something else.

Question 6 is designed to explore the abuser's self-image, self-esteem, and ego strength. We want to understand the perpetrator's self-identification, identification with others, and desires to change. Be careful about putting a candidate with no ego strength into a group as confrontive as this one. The individual may not be able to withstand so direct an approach until achieving a better ability to differentiate between self and others, between the crime and self-value. Remember that one of the initial stages the group members pass through is depression. An already severely depressed individual is not a good group candidate.

Question 7. During the interview, the counselors explained that a stipulation for admission to the group was the members openly share the details of their crime with other group members. Some were very tentative about making a commitment to do this, but firm reminders that public disclosure is prerequisite to group membership and assurance that all group members share the common bond of being incarcerated for a sexual abuse crime helped them to commit to disclose in the group.

Questions 8 and 9. Once the candidates' sexual crimes had been described in detail, individual expectations were discussed. The counselors made it very clear that the reasons for facilitating the group were to help them become aware of their feelings, to re-educate them concerning their victim or victims, and to help them begin to realistically confront the dysfunctional patterns in their lives.

A common response to questions about motivation for participating in an incest treatment group was for the inmates to say they did not know why they wanted to participate, although these responses varied from "I don't know" to tearful silence in response to the pain the question evoked. Approximately 80 percent of the perpetrators said during the initial interview that they wanted to discover why they had committed the abuse.

Initial Group Meeting

Group therapy for the offenders utilized a structured and confrontive approach. Confrontation was used to take power away from the perpetrator. In the incestuous family, it is common for the perpetrator to wield total control and power over the victim and other family members, in some cases for many years. This power position enables the perpetrator to maintain the family dysfunction that perpetuates the abuse. The inmate cannot be allowed to operate the same way in group. The facilitator establishes his or her position of power by keeping the group very structured initially and by setting rules for group behavior for which sanctions are delineated. Sex offenders typically operate from positions of power engendered by differences in size, age, role, and influence. It is important that the dichotomy is broken in the therapy setting and that the therapist operates from a firm power base in confronting the offender (Sgroi, 1982). If the offender maintains an illusion of power in the group, this power will be used defensively to recreate the same kind of dysfunction that existed in the offender's family. If the therapist allows the group to get caught up in the same kind of dynamics the perpetrator created elsewhere, that perpetrator will be enabled rather than helped. The therapist must be strong enough to remain immune to power plays.

Those of you working in prison settings have help from the system in setting up a power hierarchy: the perpetrator is the inmate, you are the person in authority—there isn't much question about it, and if there is, there is an armed guard outside your door to make things clear. Use that system to your advantage. In nonprison settings, you may have to use court mandates, the threat of incarceration, or similar tactics to gain the power advantage. It may sound harsh to those of us who are accustomed to practicing from a client-centered perspective, but in this therapeutic realm, it is important that the offender be stripped of the ability to overpower and intimidate.

The first agenda item for the initial meeting of the group is for all members to describe their crimes. This is often a highly charged emotional experience for the abusers. It was not unusual for one of the counselors to offer appropriate reassurances, sometimes touching the offenders gently or giving verbal reassurance that we care about them, and understand how difficult this experience is for them, and supporting them as they gain new insights about themselves. This retelling of the abusive act sometimes required early confrontation by the counselor. For example:

> Terry, a 46-year old white man stated that he had committed the crime but it was his wife's fault. Explaining further, Terry had sexually abused his nine-year-old daughter. He was a truck driver who came home on weekends, and said he needed sex. In his words, "My wife would go to Bingo on Friday nights instead of being with me. Naturally I turned to my daughter. I know it was wrong now, but if my wife had stayed home where she belonged I might not have done it." It took six group sessions (each two hours in length) for Terry to realize he alone was responsible for his daughter's abuse. In providing a context for the confrontation it was important to reassure the group members that the group leader cared about each of them and did not want them to hurt their children anymore. In this case, the counselor asked Terry why he didn't masturbate or go to a prostitute rather than abuse his daughter. Alternatives were explored until Terry realized he had been looking for a loving relationship and had deceived himself by thinking he could have such a relationship with a child. Terry appeared to move into a reactive depression and cried in group for the next four sessions. He felt that castration might be the only answer for men like himself.

As the first group meeting begins, the perpetrators are told the rules of the group (the confidentiality requirement, two-hour sessions every week, regular attendance, disclosure at first session, naming victims, respectful language and behavior, respect for property, and procedure for withdrawing or being terminated from group) and are told how their victims may be feeling and what they may be experiencing as a result of the abuse. The education and sensitization process begins right here. The importance of the perpetrator claiming sole responsibility is emphasized. As counselors, it is important for us to take a firm, clear, and direct stand on the nature of the abuse (interestingly, later on in the process several perpetrators verbalized that they wanted the group leader to be tough and confrontive. When asked why, they said it helped them to realize how wrong they had been.)

The leader insists the victims be called by name in order to humanize them, and that the perpetrator tell as many of the details necessary to describe the crime. The majority of those in the groups, without further urging, both named their victims and told specifically the crime they had been charged with. Most did not give specific details in the first session. The counselor needs to be encouraging, supportive, and understanding, yet firm that disclosure is a very important part of the group process.

A sense of relief commonly follows self-disclosure, and group cohesiveness develops quickly. Surprisingly to the counselors, all the offenders attended subsequent sessions expectantly. Even though group participation was voluntary, absence from the group was rare. By revealing details of each person's crime to fellow group members, the "secret" was taken away, and the issues could be approached realistically. As the first group meeting concluded, the counselor assigned homework. For example, if self-identification is the problem, an autobiography is assigned. Often the perpetrators are asked to write a list of reasons they had abused the child. (Chapter 3 elaborates on homework assignments.) For some, the initial group is so traumatic that homework is not given. A "pep talk," encouraging participation, is given in the last fifteen minutes to "defuse" the group. Be sure to use some time to stroke the group members for risking by participating. Express your respect for a well-done piece of therapeutic work. Encourage members to be honest. Assure them you are there to help them; that you have heard it all and that they do not need to protect or take care of you. Challenge them to take care of themselves by doing what they need to do in group so they will not go back out into the world and do something harmful to someone else. And always put the responsibility for their healing on them: "It's your work. I can't do it for you. But I'm here because I'm willing to help you do it for yourselves. It's up to you to decide whether you are going to make changes or not. Changes require work. I'll help you work on making changes, but you have to do the work."

Development of Personal Responsibility

We have talked about responsibility throughout this book. In this section, we will briefly sketch some related treatment issues. It is very important that the development of personal responsibility begins during the initial interview. Unless it is specifically required that the inmates own their incestuous behavior, as it is for a program of treatment such as ours, perpetrators of sexual crimes may complete the entire period of incarceration without ever discussing the crime! If you cannot even get to the crime, how will you get to the shame, the lost self-esteem, the anger, and the behavioral response to those feelings that perpetuate the offensive behavior? Be firm in order that the tone for subsequent sessions is set right from the beginning.

The relationship of the perpetrator to the victim must be clearly defined ("she was my daughter") and a factual detailed description of the crime must be elicited from the perpetrator and then restated by the counselor. For example, "You put your penis in your daughter Sally's mouth." Graphic restatement is necessary in order to help the perpetrator experience the full impact of the abusive behavior. When the perpetrators hear the restatement, they are often shocked at their own behavior. New insights often occur after such an eye-opening experience.

It is imperative that the counselor work with the perpetrators to see what was occurring in their early life in order to learn whether the crime is related to their childhood experience. Remember to enforce the notion that experience is no excuse for irresponsible response. We create our responses to our experiences and are "response-able" for them.

The theme of responsibility needs to be played consistently throughout treatment. During disclosures and in other interchanges, the counselor needs to be prepared to refocus on the victim. Acceptance of responsibility for the offense does not seem to occur until the perpetrator can describe the victim as a fully faceted, fully feeling, and individualized person. Humanizing the victim prepares the way for the perpetrator to take responsibility for the abuse. Encourage the perpetrator to describe the victim as from afar. Do a visualization exercise in which the perpetrator watches the victim play with other children or interact with other adults and describes the victim's looks, actions, interactions with other people, how others respond to the victim, how the victim responds to others, how the victim responds to the perpetrator, what are the victim's strong points, fears, likes and dislikes, talents, individuality, what the victim needs from his or her parents, what the victim needed from the perpetrator—and what was received instead. Help the perpetrators to overcome the tendency to see the victim as an object for their self-expression and to see instead the victim as a child hurt, frightened, betrayed, and defiled by their behavior.

Working Through Issues Emerging From Assuming Responsibility

When offenders can finally acknowledge the enormity of the impact of the sexual abuse they inflicted on the child, they tend to become depressed and fear that neither they nor the child may ever recover from the trauma.

The counselors work with this hopelessness by assigning homework. An invaluable tool is letter writing. Start the letter "Dear Daddy" or some similar applicable salutation. Instruct the offenders to write the letters as if they were the child. You may even want to dictate the first sentence: "I want to forgive you for what you did to me, but. . . ." This technique facilitates awareness of how damaging their behavior has been and forces the abusers to fully confront the consequences of the abuse from the victim's perspective. Starting the letter with an intent to forgive diffuses some of the hopelessness and focuses the content on what needs to be done in order for forgiveness to occur. Letters may be rewritten as many times as necessary until the perpetrators fully understand the impact of their behavior on the child, express remorse, and resolve to change their behavior. The group counselors firmly believe that perpetrators must eventually talk to or write to their victim(s) and attempt, by accepting full responsibility, to relieve any guilt the child might be experiencing. Writing therapeutic letters such as we have described helped the group members to feel they had a means to do something to rectify some modicum of the emotional upheaval caused by the abuse. The awareness that they can take an active role in the healing of the victim and the family helps to relieve some of the helpless-hopeless dynamics that contribute to the depression and suicide risk. Use the same technique to help put them in the place of the nonoffending parent, sibling, or other involved person. Use it also in addressing their own victimization: have them write to their own abuser. Then have them reply from the abuser's perspective and compare their letter from their abuser to their letter to their victim. Use the two responses to draw parallels and differences between what was done to them and what they did to another.

The process of reading and rewriting these letters was supplemented with role-play. Often the issue of the perpetrators' relationship with their spouse was brought out, highlighting the fact that the spouse was also victimized. Although initially most perpetrators cannot understand this perspective, role-playing in conjunction with letter writing developed awareness and insight. Again, it must be mentioned that confrontation is essential in this stage of the therapy.

In order to give you a sense of the impact that these letters have, we will share an excerpt from a letter one perpetrator wrote to his wife as he struggled to understand how she was impacted by his incestuous behavior:

Sue: I hope you don't mind my writing you this letter. Somehow deep down inside I feel I'll never see you again. I really can't explain it. All I know is that I caused you both the pain and shame that no one should have to bear. I understand more and more of my selfish judgments and my neurotic behavior all through my life. It is only now that I'm beginning to understand the reasons why. It's painful to accept my own ignorance, but I hurt more for what I've done to you and Sheri than I could ever hurt from being in prison. . . . There are many moments that I cry because I'm afraid that you will never forgive me. I become depressed because of what I did to you and Sheri and everything, as I do not want to live. . . . I understand how careless

I lived and how little I knew of what the consequences were for all of us. Now I have to understand and live with what I have done. . . . I've ruined your lives and I'm sorry. . . .

The clients confront not only the therapist, but also their own behavior. In the example above, the perpetrator, by being required to assume the vantage point of his wife, was forced to give up the denial he had maintained up to that point and confront the pain caused by his offensive behavior. The therapist was confrontive in insisting that he in turn confront the consequences of his behavior as his wife sees them.

Re-education and Sensitization

Re-education and sensitization may, for these perpetrators, be a misnomer. We found that most of the perpetrators needed initial education and sensitization. Most had no concept of the pain, hurt, or distrust they had caused— or even that their victims were capable of these feelings. Most of the efforts during this phase of the group were directed at having the perpetrators describe times when they had experienced intense feelings of hurt, pain, or distrust, and assisting them to explore those experiences and to apply the insights to their victims. One inmate, victimized by an uncle, perpetrated the exact crime on his son. When asked how he felt when committing the crime, since he had a personal experience with sexual abuse, he was overwhelmed. He had never transposed his feelings as a victim to his victim's experience. The use of films and bringing in an adult victim of sexual abuse was useful in helping the perpetrator confront a victim, obtain an education from the victim's perspective, and to become sensitized to the victim's experience. (See case example "Christine" in chapter 1.)

No one will be surprised to hear that education and sensitization are processes. It will also surprise no one to hear that counselors and therapists are also teachers. As therapists we are constantly educating and re-educating, sensitizing and resensitizing. The most productive group therapists are those who are constantly listening for deficits. In your work with perpetrators, as in your work with any other population, look for the deficits, and assume that the person identifying the deficit is not the only group member who needs to be educated but is merely the only group member willing to ask to be educated. Then, educate them. The educational topics will vary according to the members, their experience, and the setting. Some of the educational deficits we found in our work with incarcerated perpetrators were: understanding of the loss and grief process; existence of a feelings vocabulary; ability to identify and refine feelings; awareness of the effect of their incarceration on the family; ability to understand the victim's perspective; basic understanding of the legal process involved in case management; basic understanding of family dynamics, parenting roles, and child development.

Termination of Group Therapy

The last few sessions were spent talking about alternative means of dealing with stress once released from the facility. Contingency plans were made for dealing with situations and feelings when the group was no longer accessible for support. All members not eligible for parole or release wanted to participate in second generation groups and were integrated wherever possible as "peer counselors." This worked out exceptionally well, since it helped build the trust necessary for the next group and served to reinforce issues already worked through.

We hope that we have convinced you that the work can be done and have given you a picture of what the work looks like. Now that you are eager to begin, you may be wondering what you need to do to get started. Once you have an idea about how you would approach therapy with perpetrators and have credentialed treatment professionals ready to provide group therapy, you need to find a host facility—either an agency or a correctional facility. Because treatment for perpetrators may be an idea new to the agency or facility, you will need to sell them on the need for treatment and give them your idea of what you propose to do. The next section provides a framework for getting started.

Getting Started in Group Treatment

One of our objectives for writing this book is to provide for your use some of the tools we had to create for ourselves. This section provides you with a program proposal you can use as a starting place for developing your own proposal for starting a group for incarcerated perpetrators of incest, or for the basis of a funding grant for group work. We offer these tools as a gift: take what you want and leave the rest. This program proposal is based on the realities of the system *as it now is*, not on the ideal system of services that we proposed in chapter 4.

Developing a Program Proposal

The first thing you are going to need is patience. Whenever you are trying to do something new and different, the recipients of your service are going to want to move slowly and carefully. Especially in the corrections system, things change slowly. Remember when working with correctional facilities that their first priority is security, not therapy. Be prepared to work within their security-oriented framework. That framework imposes some limitations on what you can do. You need to be prepared to fully comply with all their security policies, including security orientation, regulations about moving around inside the facility, time constraints, and space constraints. Laying the foundation for work within correctional facilities takes considerable time, so be prepared to invest a great deal of lead-time.

The proposal we are sharing with you was one developed for a correctional facility. The same proposal can be modified for submission to a human service agency.

We see a great need for group and individual support services to help the offender make the transition back to family and community after leaving the correctional facility. Grant monies are a possible source of funding for such support services. Most inmates being released through parole have a job lined up when they are discharged. Those released at their max date, without parole supervision, may or may not have a job prospect. At any rate, these people have a lot of catching up to do. They need to find a place to live, transportation, a way to feed and clothe themselves. In most cases, they want to leave the prison experience far behind. They have little or no money when they are returned to the community, are highly motivated to obtain money, and are not motivated to spend it on therapy. Survival needs take first priority. If we are to provide consistent community support services for former sex offenders, we need to find ways to fund those services. Where service providers are building a direct link between community support services for former offenders and therapeutic programs in correctional facilities, our sample program proposal may be helpful in writing grant proposals for community-based aftercare services.

A word or two about measurement instruments: You will notice that this proposal includes a section describing the measurement instrument proposed for use in data gathering and treatment effectiveness evaluation. The instrument proposed is the Fundamental Interpersonal Relations Orientation (FIRO) Awareness Scales. As the proposal states, this instrument battery was selected because it measures variables that are applicable to treatment issues, is easy to use and to score, is easy to administer, is useful in providing comparison data over several measurement periods, and has proven reliability and validity. You may find another instrument to be more useful for your work. Be sure you investigate available instruments carefully before you invest time, money, and energy in a longitudinal study to which you are committed for an extended period of time. The point is, we need to make sure we are measuring useful and meaningful aspects of behavior and attitudes that are going to produce useful and meaningful descriptions and inferences. The FIRO Awareness Scales are available to licensed psychologists through the American Psychological Association (APA). Unless you are a licensed psychologist, to use this instrument or any other psychometric device controlled by the APA, you will need the endorsement of a psychologist. Usually the agency or correctional facility will have a psychologist on staff who can review your program plans with you, approve your selection of an instrument, order it for you, and supervise instrument administration and subsequent evaluation of collected data.

The program proposal may be your first contact with the agency or correctional facility, or may be delivered to the agency or facility in response to an initial inquiry about interest in developing a treatment or support program. While you may wish to make your program less-structured than the one outlined in this proposal, we suggest your proposal reflect this kind of structure in order to communicate that you know what you are doing, that you have a program design in mind, and that the first treatment program has a termination point at which treatment effectiveness can be evaluated and a decision can be made about continuing with a second-generation program. This also gives you an "out" in case you choose not to continue the program or feel the need to modify the program before running it again. When you get into face-to-face planning with the facility or agency administration, you can modify your program proposal to mutual benefit.

Be aware that once offenders make an investment in the program, they may find it hard to surrender. For some, this group will be their first experience with understanding and compassionate human beings. For some, it will be the first time they have been able to let their defenses down enough to experiment with being understanding and compassionate. Group members will grow rapidly once they can shed their defenses and begin making changes in their lives. They develop a sense of safety with fellow group members. They develop a sense of unconditional positive regard: no matter what they confess, or do, or say, they know they are valued as people even when the group disapproves of their behavior. Doesn't all this describe a functional family? For some, it will be hard to leave the group when its work is complete, and they will want to stay on for another generation of group work. If you get started with this work and then leave—for whatever reason—you need to be prepared to deal with the anger, loss, disappointment, disorientation, and possible ambivalence of the group before you go. Whether you are a volunteer facilitator or a paid service provider, these clients come to depend on you to take them through the process. As treatment providers who are also teachers and models, we need to make sure we behave responsibly with our clients.

Sample Program Proposal

Program Proposal for Group Treatment for Incarcerated Perpetrators of Incest or Incest-like Offenses

Purpose and Philosophy of the Proposed Program

Social work, psychology, psychiatry, counseling, pop literature, and media reports are full of horror stories about the effects of sexual abuse on children and adults who survive the experience. These stories are not overblown. Personal therapeutic experience with victims of sexual abuse attests that the damage is more hideous, the scars deeper, and the effects more long-lasting than the stories indicate. Conservatively, one in four girls, one in seven boys, and one in ten families experience the nightmare of child sexual abuse. Our society is now providing compensation for treatment to victims of sexual abuse—treatment that is long overdue. But the story is quite different for the perpetrator.

With few exceptions, adjudicated perpetrators of sexual abuse "end up" in jail. The tragic truth of the matter is that they do not "end up" in confinement. They are paroled or they complete their sentence and are released back into the population *untreated.* So while we are pretty good at punishing them for what they have done, we have not sufficiently modified their behavior to assure society that the offender will not repeat the offense with another child, maybe yours or mine. We release the perpetrators with the understanding that "they have paid their debt to society," return them, with all the same dysfunctional coping habits they brought with them, to the same environment that fostered their offensive behavior in the first place, and leave them alone without workable tools to rebuild their lives. Many perpetrators do just that—they *rebuild* their lives complete with the same repertoire of dysfunctional behaviors that predisposed them to the offensive behavior in the first place. We need only look at the staggering recidivism rate for sex offenders to confirm this.

Professionals working with victims are willing to settle for no less than full healing and recovery for the child. Yet, traditionally, we have been satisfied with treating the child victim, neglecting the fact that the perpetrator is a part of that child's family and emotional environment for life. For the sake of the victim, we believe the perpetrator, and indeed the entire family, must be treated as well. In order for the victim's healing to be complete, the perpetrator must sincerely and independently take full responsibility for the abusive behavior and communicate that to the victim, thus relieving the child of culpability. The objective in family work with incestuous families is to reduce the emotional residue of the abusive event to the point where the abuse can be placed into a manageable life context rather than being allowed to dominate or to define the victim; to work through the pain to the point where both the victim and the perpetrator are able to say, "Yes, it happened; and it was horrible, but I am not limited to defining myself or my life in terms of that trauma. I have learned from it and now I am ready and able to move on."

The lasting effects of sexual abuse on the victim are well-documented—one needs only to pick up a magazine to read about them. But there are also consequences for the untreated perpetrator: social isolation; alienation from family, community, and profession or workplace; continued destruction of self-esteem; continued abuse; and bi-directional abuse. Research is confirming that the cycle of victimization works in both directions. Not only is an abusive adult likely to abuse his or her children who are weaker and more vulnerable, the abuser is also likely to perpetuate the abuse backward to the previous generation: to abuse the frail, elderly parent who probably taught the abusing behavior by example. The cycle is likely to repeat and repeat, generating bi-directional abuse throughout generations of families. All these residual effects make it difficult if not impossible to transform the offender from an inmate to a productive member of society and to ensure the safety of potential victims.

Experience and research have revealed that most abusers were themselves abused. They are adults with dysfunctional learning histories upon which are built systems of dysfunctional responses to anxiety and stress. If we can provide a therapeutic environment for working on the unresolved pain of this dysfunctional history, if we can break through the defenses that separate the perpetrator from owning the abusive behavior, bring the perpetrator to a full cognitive and emotional understanding of the consequences of the abusive behavior, build new repertoires of responses, and help the perpetrator see the need for, and provide tools for, constructing supportive post-incarceration resources, we may be able to begin to interrupt the cycle of intergenerational abuse. It's a tall order, but we need to find an opening and make a start.

Proposal

We propose a program of professional group treatment for incarcerated offenders of incest or incest-like crimes, facilitated by one or two trained professionals. Groups consist of four to ten inmates and one to two facilitators. (Where treatment groups for offenders of rape are to be established, participation of a qualified corrections counselor may be required as co-facilitator.) Group sessions last two hours and meet once per week during regularly scheduled program hours. Duration of treatment is twenty-two to thirty-eight weeks. Groups meet inside the facility and are visually monitored by security personnel in the same manner as are any other facility programs. Facilitators are trained, experienced group therapists who comply with the facility's security and orientation requirements.

Program Objectives

Objectives of the proposed program are five-fold:

1. to prevent re-offense;
2. to facilitate healing of the victim, the family, and the community;
3. to create awareness of and intervene in the family dysfunction that spawned the abusive behavior;
4. to enable the perpetrator to build a new and more fully functioning life, void of offensive behaviors, following release from incarceration; and
5. to provide means of data collection intended for research, treatment effectiveness, and behavior-change-monitoring purposes.

Referral of Inmates for Group Treatment

Prospective group members are to be recommended by corrections counselors, chaplains, and other staff members based upon the inmate's case history and/or expressed desire to participate in an incest-specific treatment program.

Candidates are to be screened by the treatment professionals, interviewed, and evaluated for group treatment appropriateness. The treatment providers have final authority in determining which candidates will be accepted for treatment. No inducements, rewards, or endorsements will be offered to prospective group members in exchange for participation in treatment. Treatment is entirely voluntary and conditional only on signature of Informed Consent for Treatment.

Requirements for Program Eligibility

The ideal prospective group member meets the following criteria (criteria may be modified per the professional judgment of the treatment professionals):

1. must be twenty-one years old or older;
2. must be thirty-four or more weeks from discharge from the facility;
3. must have been physically nonviolent during the instant offense;
4. must be willing to commit to participate fully (attend all group meetings for the duration of the treatment program);
5. must be functionally literate;
6. must be substance-free;
7. must be free of severe, disabling psychopathology;
8. must be willing to participate in three individual screening sessions with one or more of the therapists prior to the first group meeting;
9. must be willing to describe the instant offense in detail at the first group session;
10. must consent to submitting to a written, standardized measurement instrument designed to gather data on treatment effectiveness, which will be administered three times over the course of treatment and release; and
11. must provide written informed consent both for treatment and for the use of the measurement instrument.

Measurement Instrument to Be Used for Data Gathering*

As of this writing, the FIRO Awareness Scales are the proposed instrument of choice. These validity and reliability tested scales consist of a battery of written questions for which the subject provides written response by circling an answer on a prepared answer sheet. The battery measures aspects of Fundamental Interpersonal Relationship Orientation that the treatment providers believe to be relevant to the treatment of incest behavior. Specific subscales to be used are named and described as follows (information is taken from the FIRO Manual):

FIRO-B (Fundamental Interpersonal Relations Orientation—Behavior): A measure of a person's characteristic behavior toward other people in the areas of inclusion, control, and affection. It is designed not only to measure individual characteristics, but also to assess expectations for relationships between people, such as compatibility or coefficiency.

FIRO-F (Fundamental Interpersonal Relations Orientation—Feelings): A measure of a person's characteristic feelings toward others. This instrument is parallel to FIRO-B. It measures the feeling level rather than the behavior level. The dimensions paralleling inclusion, control, and affection are (respectively): significance, competence, and loveability. FIRO-F is designed to measure interaction as well as individual traits.

LIPHE (Life Interpersonal History Enquiry): A measure of the retrospective account of the respondent's relations with his or her parents before age six. LIPHE measures these relations in the areas of inclusion, control, and affection, and at the levels of behavior and of feelings. There are separate scales for the respondent's relationship with father and with mother. LIPHE measures only the respondent's report of these relations, without assuming the accuracy of this report.

MATE (Marital Attitudes Evaluation): Originally a measure of satisfaction of husband with wife and wife with husband on inclusion, control, and affection at the levels of behavior and feelings, MATE was revised to apply to any pair of persons in close contact with each other regardless of marital contract.

COPE (Coping Operations Preference Enquiry): A measure of the respondent's preference for certain types of defense or coping mechanisms. Respondent is given a series of situations based on the various types of interpersonal anxiety suggested by the FIRO theory and a choice of reactions to these situations, all phrased in terms of defenses and presented in a semi-projective format. The respondent must then express a preference among denial, isolation, projection, regression-dependency, and turning-against-self.

Each scale is relatively short and can be completed in a few minutes by subjects of average intelligence and language ability. The vocabulary required is simple. Arrangements will be made to assist nonreaders or remedial readers to complete the scales. The items are nonthreatening and do not arouse feelings of invasion of privacy in the completer. The scales are self-administering, and scoring is a simple, rapid clerical operation with instructions provided on scoring templates. The scores produced by the various scales are relatively easy to interpret because they are based on the same number of items. Since their publication in the late 1960s and early 1970s, the FIRO Awareness Scales have achieved widespread use and are evaluated in psychometric literature.

The FIRO Awareness Scales have been chosen for use in this treatment program and data-gathering not only for their validity and reliability, but also because the scales address the therapeutic issues raised in treatment for perpetrators of incest and incest-like behavior. The program designers believe that comparison of pretreatment, posttreatment, and follow-up measures will not only provide data on treatment effectiveness, but will also provide a means of monitoring treatment endurance.

The theory behind FIRO is based on the assumption that all human interaction may be divided into three categories: issues surrounding inclusion, control, and affection. The FIRO theory of group development states that a group proceeds through inclusion issues into control issues and finally into affection issues; then it recycles. To illustrate these issues, the FIRO Manual makes an analogy to a group of people riding in a boat. Inclusion is the decision whether or not be included on the boatride. Control refers to who is directing and maneuvering the boat. Affection refers to any close relationships that develop among pairs of people. Inclusion, control, and affection are measured in two dimensions each: expressed (what the individual expresses to others) and wanted (what the individual wants from others).

FIRO scores can be used to monitor progress in therapy, to measure a degree of change from the baseline (pretreatment) measure to periodic or posttreatment measures, and to measure the maintenance or extinction of any change over a postrelease period following incarceration. Ultimately, should sufficient data be collected and correlations found, the scales have potential for predicting postincarceration recidivism.

A Specimen Set can be made available for examination. Instruments must be ordered by a psychologist authorized to order materials from the American Psychological Association.

Intent and Projected Use of Data

Treatment for perpetrators of sex crimes is relatively new, both within and outside correctional facilities. As is the case with any developing science, we need to collect empirical data on the efficacy of treatment in order to begin to identify and refine treatment methods and techniques that can be proven to produce durable behavior change. The treatment program herein proposed is an approach to therapy for incarcerated incest perpetrators that intends to simultaneously provide (1) unilateral, systemic treatment of the dysfunctional family and (2) direct, confrontive group treatment for incarcerated offenders. Data collected will be used to measure treatment effectiveness and treatment duration. Data will be securely stored, anonymous (identifiable only by a symbol of the inmate's devising), and treated with the utmost confidentiality. Results will be analyzed and used for research and training purposes, and may form the basis of a doctoral thesis and/or a published volume intended to train professional workers and influence treatment policy. Subjects will never be identified by name or any other identifying characteristics.

No data will be collected without first obtaining voluntary Informed Consent and signed Consent to Release Confidential Information.

Control Group

Control group population will consist of candidates who have expressed interest in receiving treatment, but who are not actively receiving treatment (waiting-list status).

Group Composition

Four group members to one facilitator, or eight to ten group members to two facilitators (to be determined by facility policy, demand for treatment, available meeting space, and facilitator availability).

Group members will be selected by the therapist/facilitators from the candidates proposed by the facility staff, interviewed, and screened for group appropriateness.

Group Treatment Plan

PHASE I: INDIVIDUAL COUNSELING COMPONENT (3–5 weeks)

Before the first group meeting, individual group candidates will meet with one or more facilitators as follows:

Session 1: Screening Interview

- presentation and signature of Informed Consent for Treatment form;
- presentation and signature of Informed Consent for Participation in a Research Study form;
- presentation and signature of Release of Confidential Information form (to enable use of data for publication or training).

Session 2: Initial Evaluation

- administration of standardized measurement instruments.

Session 3:

- administration of standardized measurement instruments.

Additional Sessions:

- additional individual counseling sessions will be provided on an as-needed and as-requested basis as time and facilities allow;

- time and place for such sessions will be negotiated with the Counseling and Security staff of the facility.

PHASE II: GROUP COUNSELING COMPONENT (18–30 weeks)

Module 1 (6–10 weeks): Development of Personal Responsibility

- breaking through denial and resistance;
- humanizing the victim;
- taking responsibility for the offensive behavior;
- anger, power, and control issues;
- issues relative to the abuser's own abuse.

Module 2 (6–10 weeks): Re-education and Sensitization

- understanding the damage done to the victim and the nonvictimized family members;
- family dynamics;
- sexuality and intimacy.

Module 3 (6–10 weeks): Transition

- the process of forgiveness and healing;
- alternatives to abusive behavior;
- connecting with community-based support.

PHASE III: TERMINATION COMPONENT (1–3 sessions)

- administration of standardized measurement instrument;
- follow-up and resolution of residual issues;
- referral to community-based aftercare and support services;
- informed consent to maintain contact for administration of six-month posttreatment;
- administration of standardized measurement instrument.

PHASE IV: FOLLOW-UP COMPONENT (by mail)
Mail standardized measurement instrument to former inmate with a stamped, self-addressed envelope for return of completed scales providing follow-up posttreatment data.

Projected Treatment Time (from screening to termination)

Between twenty-two and thirty-eight weeks (exclusive of holidays, vacations, and weeks during which group meetings are otherwise impossible to hold). Following completion of one group experience, group members who choose to continue through a second generation program may request permission to continue as a peer counselor with the next program.

Program Cost

Cost of Standardized Instrument	_____
Materials	_____
Equipment Costs	_____
Facility and Security Costs	_____
Counselor Remuneration	_____
Administrative Costs	_____
Clerical Costs	_____
Mailing Costs	_____
TOTAL PROJECTED COSTS	_____

Special Needs

- Videotape and audiotape recording and play-back equipment (for training);
- Group meeting room that can be monitored by security officers;
- Access to secure file storage (for instrument storage and access);
- Access to inmate case files (for screening and information confirmation);
- Clerical services (copying, typing, filing, file retrieval, gate clearance requests as needed);
- Conferral with corrections counselors as needed to ensure quality treatment.

Thank you for your interest and for your response.

Sample Research Design Proposal

As you read the sample research design proposal that follows, notice that the proposal is idealized; that is, it is a longitudinal study that continues over a five-year period. While the program proposal was based on the system as it is, the research proposal is based on an ideal: a five-year posttreatment time frame. It is a simple matter to shorten the study to a more realistic time frame (we suggest a posttreatment measure with a six-month remeasure). In reality, an inmate released from a correctional facility, may have a parole connection for up to eighteen months if released before the max date with time off for "good time," or no parole connection if the entire sentence is completed. Once the perpetrator "maxes out" of the facility or completes parole, there are no longer any connections with corrections counselors. Corrections personnel rarely interact with parole personnel. As a result (especially if there is no parole connection), once the inmate leaves the facility there is no way of maintaining contact unless the inmate volunteers that information. Even then, our experience is that once they leave the facility, they become anonymous. Very few make any kind of contact once they return to the streets. This kind of disconnection makes longitudinal study very difficult. Under the kind of service delivery system we proposed in chapter 4, a connection could be sustained, enabling us to make contact for monitoring and data collection.

We have presented the research design proposal in its idealized form with the understanding that it will need to be modified to be useful with the system as it is. We need all the data we can collect; we also need to be realistic about our expectations. We suggest you consider a pretreatment administration, a posttreatment administration, and attempt to arrange for a six-month posttreatment administration via mail. At the six-month administration you can request permission to contact the client again at six-month intervals for other administrations of the instrument.

As does the program proposal, the research design proposal utilizes the

FIRO Awareness Scales as a measurement instrument. Use the best instrument available to you that thoroughly meets your research needs.

There are a number of intervention points from which one could start to find an effective way to treat sex offenders. Some of us will elect to engage in hands-on treatment. Some will elect to advocate for treatment or legislative reform. Some readers may be more interested in designing research that will provide treatment-effectiveness data. All are viable places to start. Again, we are providing you with the product of our thinking in order to give you a starting point for your own thinking and intervention. Take whatever you find useful from this model and create from it something of your own that will take us all closer to the objective of finding effective, enduring treatment for sex offenders.

Because we do not live in an ideal world, because research designs are never without faults, and because of the current state-of-the-arts (both the art of treatment and the art of research), this model will need to be modified to meet individual needs, location, setting, available time, and materials.

Research Design for Treatment Effectiveness: Group Treatment for Incarcerated Incest Offenders

Purpose

This study intends to establish a cause and effect relationship between a treatment program for incarcerated incest or incest-like offenders and successful rehabilitation.

The program in question is for treatment of incest and incest-like offenders at a medium security New York State correctional facility. If proven effective in successfully rehabilitating incest offenders, group treatment programs for offenders could become a commonly accepted component of correctional programming. Additionally, the proposed research project intends to gather enough information to yield additional data on whether there is carryover to postincarceration functioning in the community, whether the effect of treatment is durable over time or diminishes over time, and over a five-year period, whether any diminishment of effect occurs. Such information may help practitioners develop more effective support services for offenders after release from prison. One objective of treatment is to sustain the "correction" incurred during incarceration and to prevent recurrence of the offensive behavior. Aside from the physical, emotional, and developmental cost to victims, the cost of treatment may far outweigh the cost of continuing offense, arrest, adjudication, and incarceration.

Literature Review

Review of the literature indicated no existing research that seeks to establish a cause and effect relationship between an incest-specific treatment program for incarcerated offenders and success of rehabilitation of incestuous molesters. No study used rehabilitation criteria broader than recidivism alone. An empirical study of treatment effectiveness was carried out in 1978 to evaluate the impact of the Child Sexual Abuse Treatment Program directed by Henry Giarretto in Santa Clara County, California. That program is a multi-faceted outpatient treatment program. Measurement was conducted on forty-four separate indices of change (including recidivism), taken at three measurement points.

Some theorists assert that apprehension, adjudication, and incarceration are in themselves rehabilitating (Sgroi, 1982; MacDonald, 1971). One is left to ask whether perceived success in rehabilitation is attributable to treatment or whether it is the result of the general prison experience. This study seeks to find a distinction between these two possible sources of attribution and, additionally, between incest-specific treatment and nonincest-specific treatment.

While reduction of recidivism is an appropriate goal for an agency of the criminal justice system, there is indication in the literature that recidivism alone may not be an adequate or appropriate measure of rehabilitation (Groth, 1978, 1982; Brecher, 1978).

Conceptual Framework

The proposed research deals with two variables of interest: the independent variable is the treatment condition, the dependent variable is rehabilitation. The researcher predicts finding that offenders who participate in incest-specific treatment will display more successful rehabilitation over a five-year period than will offenders who participate in a nonincest-specific treatment program. Furthermore, rehabilitation for both treatment conditions is expected to be more successful than for those in the nontreatment condition. In short, we expect to find that incest-specific treatment significantly enhances the success of rehabilitation.

General Research Hypothesis

The proposed research seeks to gain evidence to indicate the incest-specific treatment program in question directly contributes to the successful rehabilitation of incest offenders to a statistically more significant degree than does nonincest-specific treatment, or than does incarceration alone without treatment. Three hypotheses are proposed:

H1: Incest offenders who participate in incest-specific treatment experience a more successful degree of rehabilitation over a five-year period than incest offenders who participate in nonincest-specific treatment.

H2: Incest offenders who participate in nonincest-specific treatment experience a more successful degree of rehabilitation over a five-year period than incest offenders who elect no treatment.

H3: Incest offenders who participate in incest-specific treatment experience a more successful degree of rehabilitation over a five-year period than incest offenders who elect no treatment.

Operational Definitions

For the purpose of the proposed study, *treatment* refers to one of the three treatment conditions an identified offender can choose from.

Operational Definitions of the Three Treatment Conditions

Incest-specific treatment refers to an existing psychotherapeutically oriented group designed to confront and address issues that predisposed the offender to incestuous act(s). This group focuses on issues such as admitting the commission of the crime, assuming full responsibility for the crime and its consequences, telling the facilitators and other group members about each incestuous act in detail, recognizing the predisposing/contributing factors that precipitated the incest, openly absolving the victim of any responsibility for the incest and asking the victim for forgiveness, recognizing personal need and developing plans for appropriate means of need satisfaction, improving self-awareness and self-image, increasing tolerance for frustration, improving impulse control, seeking means of victim compensation, exploring the offender's own childhood victimization, and recognizing and accepting the need for lifelong treatment. At this time the existing incest-specific treatment group consists of eight to ten volunteer adult male inmates proposed by their corrections counselors because of the incidence of one or more occurrences of incest in the inmate's offense history. After being apprised of the nature of both the incest-specific treatment group and the alternative nonincest-specific group (a group dealing with interpersonal relationships), and of the inmate's freedom to choose one of the two or neither, those who choose to join the incest-specific treatment group will be screened for severe psychopathology before being admitted to the group. The group is facilitated by two trained treatment professionals (one male and one female).

Nonincest-specific treatment refers to an existing psychotherapeutically oriented group designed to improve relationships of its members, especially relationships with significant women. This group focuses on issues such as understanding the differences and similarities between men and women, active listening skills, communications training, human development, parenting skills, parenting styles, human sexuality, changing marital roles, stress management, and personal problem solving. The existing relationships group consists of eight to ten volunteer adult male inmates proposed by their corrections counselors because of the incidence of one or more occurrences of incest in the inmate's offense history. After being apprised of the nature of both the incest-specific treatment group and the alternative nonincest-specific group (a group dealing with interpersonal relationships) and of the inmate's freedom to choose one of the two or neither, those who choose to join the relationships group will be screened for severe psychopathology before being admitted to the group. The group is facilitated by two trained treatment professionals (one male, one female).

No treatment refers to the third treatment condition in which inmates proposed by their corrections counselors because of the incidence of one or more occurrences of incest in the inmate's offense history. After being apprised of the nature of both the incest-specific treatment group and the alternative nonincest-specific group (a group dealing with interpersonal relationships) and of the inmate's freedom to choose one of the two or neither, those who choose to join neither group will be assigned to the *no-treatment* group. In comprising a control group, inmates electing the no-treatment condition will be screened for severe psychopathology before being returned to the general prison environment.

No other psychotherapeutic treatment groups exist. Consenting subjects in any of the three treatment conditions will consent in writing to participation as research subjects, stipulating they have given informed consent.

Additional Operational Definitions

For the purpose of this study, *rehabilitation* refers to the inmate/offender's scores on the FIRO Awareness Scales, an instrument used to measure factors that experts in the field identify as treatment and rehabilitation issues for this population. The researcher asserts, and the literature confirms, that measurements of change on such therapeutic issues constitute a better indication of rehabilitation than recidivism alone. These measures are described in more detail in the Data Collection Methods section of this proposal. *Successful rehabilitation* refers to a notable improvement in score on the FIRO Scales between pretreatment measurements and posttreatment measurements monitored over a five-year period. *Incest offenders* is operationalized as inmates incarcerated at the correctional facility who have been identified by their corrections counselors as having one or more occurrences of incest in the inmate's offense history. These inmates will not necessarily have been adjudicated for an incest crime, but have either a criminal record of incest or have admitted to having performed incestuous acts. *Incest* is operationalized as intergenerational sexual activity between family members, particularly between a perpetrator of or above the age of eighteen and a victim under the age of eighteen.

Research Design

As presented in figure 5–1, the proposed research is designed to identify a cause and effect relationship between the independent and the dependent variables. It is a field experiment of quasi-experimental design. The study is longitudinal in time frame and follows a Nonequivalent Comparison Group configuration with repeated posttreatment measures. Because the study seeks to compare differences between programs that already exist and for which voluntary participation is required, random assignment to treatment conditions is not possible.

We propose to study inmates at the identified New York State correctional facility who have a history of incest and have elected one of the three treatment conditions already outlined. Each inmate will complete the FIRO Awareness Scales battery twelve times over a five-year period. As an indication of Observer Reliability, the inmate's assigned corrections counselor (during the period of incarceration) and parole officer (during the period of parole) will complete the same Index of Observations about the inmate at the same intervals as the subject (ideally over a five-year period) for as long as those relationships endure. Data will be gathered as follows:

Measurement #1 will be taken after the inmate/offender elects a treat-

Figure 5-1

LONGITUDINAL RESEARCH DESIGN

	Pretreatment	Treatment	Posttreatment	Parole/Release										
				6 mos.	6 mos.	6 mos.	6 mos.	6 mos.	6 mos.	6 mos.	6 mos.	6 mos.	6 mos.
Incest-Specific Group	O_1	X	O_2	O_3	O_4	O_5	O_6	O_7	O_8	O_9	O_{10}	O_{11}	O_{12}
Nonincest-Specific Group	O_1	X	O_2	O_3	O_4	O_5	O_6	O_7	O_8	O_9	O_{10}	O_{11}	O_{12}
No-Treatment Group	O_1	X	O_2	O_3	O_4	O_5	O_6	O_7	O_8	O_9	O_{10}	O_{11}	O_{12}

1 year   1 year   1 year   1 year   1 year   1 year

ment condition, is screened, and consents to participation as a research subject, but before experiencing treatment.

Measurement #2 will be taken after the inmate/offender concludes the treatment condition, but before being released from prison.

Measurement #3 will be taken six months after release from prison at a regularly scheduled meeting with the parole officer. Should the inmate be released at the max date (with no parole), measurements will be mailed to the inmate, completed, and returned to the researcher by return mail.

Measurements #4 through #12 will be taken at six-month intervals. Instruments will be mailed to the inmate, completed, and returned to the researcher by mail. Where a relationship exists with a parole officer, instruments will be mailed to the parole officer for joint administration to subject and parole office, then returned together to the researcher by return mail. Measurements conclude at the end of a five-year period.

Data will be collected by use of the same instrument administered individually, sealed into an envelope, and returned to the researcher. Instruments completed by corrections counselors and parole officers will be sealed and returned in the same envelope as the subject's instrument, identified only by badge number so that follow-up will be possible if necessary. The offender's instrument will be identified by a symbol of the offender's choosing, known only to the offender and the researcher until the completion of the study. Returned instruments will be stored under lock and key until completion of the study.

Population and Sample

The results of the proposed research are expected to generalize to offenders who have a history of molestation type incest offenses and who are incarcerated in medium security correctional facilities in New York State.

The sample consists of offenders who have a history of molestation type incest offenses and who are incarcerated in one particular New York State correctional facility and have been identified by their corrections counselors as potential treatment participants, have chosen one of the three treatment conditions, and have consented to participation as a research subject in a longitudinal study. The subjects constitute an Availability Sample because of the small number of prospective subjects, because of the scarcity of treatment programs for incarcerated incest offenders, and because geographic constraints limit the number of facilities that can be accessed at this time.

A sample size of twenty subjects in each treatment condition is desirable. A minimum of ten subjects in each treatment condition is deemed adequate.

Projected limitations to generalizability from the sample to the population deal with conditions specific to the facility that might make it unique from other medium security correctional facilities in New York State. For example: (1) if the host facility for some reason attracts particularly skilled corrections counselors who are particularly adept at identifying occurrences of incest in an inmate's history; or (2) if the inmates incarcerated in the host facility are, for some reason, atypical of inmates in other medium security facilities in New York State; or (3) if the treatment programs at the host facility differ in quality from those existing at other similar facilities, then the conditions at this facility may not approximate those available to inmates at similar New York State correctional facilities and therefore cannot be generalized.

Data Collection Method

The FIRO Awareness Scales were selected because they address items that are indicators, as identified in the specialized literature, of relevant treatment issues. To enhance reliability, self-report data will be supplemented by observational data collected from the subject's supervisor (corrections counselor or parole officer).

The response rate will be enhanced by sending the instrument forms to the appropriate supervisor just prior to the six-month interval period and asking the offender and the supervisor to fill them out during their regularly scheduled meeting (in privacy), jointly seal both instruments into a single envelope (assuring confidentiality of information between reporters), and then return both completed instruments to the researcher via return mail. Where no supervisor is available, instruments will be mailed directly to the subject with instructions to complete the instrument and return it to the researcher expediently. A return postcard will be enclosed enabling the subject to notify the researcher of change of address.

Limitations of the Study

Ethically, random assignment to conditions cannot be made without the possibility of denying treatment to a subject who desires it. We are therefore willing to tolerate this weakness in the study, which jeopardizes replicability, generalizability, and validity. Another ethical issue is the danger imposed to a subject or the compulsion of the researcher to report it if a subject, in good faith and with assurance of anonymity, discloses the perpetration of another criminal offense that endangers the well-being of a child. How will that be handled by the researcher? Additionally, there is the issue of maintaining confidentiality of the data. Security of stored and/or computerized data must be ensured. It must also be ensured that once the subject's identifying symbol is affiliated with the subject's name and committed to paper, records are properly used and are properly destroyed when they are no longer needed.

Finally, there is an inequality between the existing treatment groups that is disturbing. At this point in the design of the research we cannot ensure that both treatment groups will be facilitated by comparable therapists or that both groups will be staffed by one male and one female therapist. Some facilities may require the presence of a corrections counselor and visual monitoring by one or more corrections officer. It is uncertain what effect these factors may have on the group experience—especially if requirements are different for the two kinds of groups. Anticipated costs are as follows:

Costs

Researcher's Remuneration   _____

Clerical Costs   _____

Cost of Instrument   _____

Mailing Costs   _____

TOTAL PROJECTED COSTS   _____

Respectfully submitted

_____

Summary

In this chapter, we have outlined a group treatment program and treatment methods for incarcerated perpetrators. We feel a need to accentuate the importance of treatment whether that treatment takes place in a secure facility or in a community-based program. We will also take advantage of another opportunity to underscore the need for lifelong treatment. We need to "market" this concept to the treatment population as well as to administrators, funding sources, and program designers. Most perpetrators come into treatment reluctantly and are all too eager to conclude treatment, call themselves "fixed," and walk out the door of your facility. If they reoffend, they can blame you for not having fixed them! For those who do not voluntarily participate in treatment (the bulk of incarcerated sex offenders), for those who sit through group sessions for the Parole Board but never invest changing their problem behavior, or for those who are never even identified as sex offenders, this is the kind of denial, blaming, and avoidance our failure to treat perpetrates on the offender, on potential victims, and on society. Not only must we treat the perpetrator, we must monitor to ensure to the best of our ability that treatment is enduring, that the perpetrator (and the family, in the case of molesters) have access to the kinds of services and support they need for recovery and safety from reoffense.

One of the ways we have found to encourage imprisoned offenders to continue treatment is to provide them with a list of experienced therapists before they leave treatment. Caution: do not include your name and number on the list unless you are willing to see that client (and the family) in individual treatment after release from the facility. You can imagine how comforting it is to have an opportunity to continue treatment with a therapist with whom you are already familiar, as opposed to starting all over with a new therapist.

Our experience has been that, grateful as the perpetrators may be walking through the gate at the end of their confinement, we never really get a sense for how effective therapy has been until they are reintegrated with the community and return to us with their family for private practice continuing care. That rarely happens. Most former inmates are so eager to put the whole experience behind them and build a new life that they want no connection with their former prison-related experiences at all—including you, the therapist they were so grateful for as they passed through the gates. During group termination, members may say emotional goodbyes, complete with earnest promises about writing, calling, and keeping in touch, but we find follow-through goes one way or the other: either we get a call within the first few months asking for an appointment, or we never hear from the perpetrator again. That is not to say that the perpetrator is not in counseling elsewhere, but with the system in its present state, with no systematic follow-up, we lose track of those who do not continue with us in private counseling. Inmates are not always able to stay close to home during incarceration. While the system accommodates to an inmate's desire to be close to home whenever possible, there is not always space in a prison near the inmate's hometown, or nearby facilities may not be of the security grade ordered by the court. Some perpetrators disappear simply because they relocate to a town too distant from the community where we practice to make communication feasible. We would be a lot more comfortable about the fate of the former inmate if there was some way to systematically monitor readjustment and ensure that a connection has been made with continuing service providers.

Chapter 4 stated our belief that continuing counseling is essential to preventing recidivism, and made some policy recommendations for establishing and supporting a system of community-based treatment and aftercare for perpetrators. Chapter 5 gave you an idea of what our group treatment program for incarcerated offenders looks like and some materials to use as idea starters for advocating for treatment or for making a proposal for starting a group in your area. Next, chapter 6 will overview three existing community-based treatment programs that might give you some ideas for alternative treatment programs for sex offenders to be used as options to imprisonment or in conjunction with incarceration to provide a more comprehensive system of "correction." We suggest you refer back to figures 4–1 and 4–2 in chapter 4 of this book to get a sense of how such treatment programs might fit into a comprehensive system of treatment services. We encourage you to contribute your own modifications and improvements to the system of services we have proposed. In order to improve services for sex offenders and their families, we need the benefit of all the ideas and all the experience we can get.

6
Community-Based Treatment for Incest Perpetrators

We have taken the position that not all perpetrators need to be incarcerated. If we do not incarcerate them, what do we do with them? It goes without saying that treatment is required, but what alternatives to incarceration do we have? Alternatives do exist. In fact, there is information available in the literature about existing treatment programs. Interested to know more about existing treatment programs that claimed some degree of success, one author undertook an investigation of active treatment programs. Following specific selection criteria, six programs described in the literature as "successful incest-specific treatment programs" in the United States were identified and compared for program components and methods of evaluating program effectiveness. Interestingly, none of the six treatment programs referred to in the literature as "successful incest-specific treatment programs" was prison-based. We can only speculate that the reason for this is that as it presently operates, the prison environment cannot provide the comprehensive system of services critical to the effective treatment of the perpetrator's family system.

In this chapter, we will describe three community-based treatment programs for perpetrators: Santa Clara County Child Sexual Abuse Treatment Program (CSATP) in San Jose, California, a large-scale program widely acclaimed in the literature for its success; Parents United/Daughters and Sons United, a self-help component of CSATP that now operates independently from CSATP on a nationwide scale; and Alpha Human Services, Inc., Minneapolis, Minnesota, a small supervised-release-from-prison program designed to treat the perpetrator behaviorally and ease community reintegration. Alpha Human Services is used as incest-specific treatment in combination with incarceration. Parents United and CSATP are used both in combination with incarceration and as an alternative to incarceration.

Santa Clara County Child Sexual Abuse Treatment Program (CSATP)

Background

In 1971, Eunice Peterson, Supervisor, and Robert S. Spitzer, M.D., consulting psychiatrist for the Juvenile Probation Department of Santa Clara County, California, invited Dr. Henry Giarretto to contribute some volunteer time for treatment of incest families. At that time, Dr. Giarretto was a practitioner of Humanistic Psychology at the Center for Human Communication in Los Gatos, specializing in family therapy. Eunice Peterson had become disenchanted with the county's method of dealing with incest families, a method she saw as being highly disruptive and destructive to the family in its effort to protect the victim and punish the perpetrator. In Dr. Spitzer's opinion, conjoint family therapy, in which Giarretto was experienced, was a promising therapeutic intervention for incest families. Thus, an eight-week trial program was begun using conjoint family therapy and based on a humanistic psychology-oriented, growth-model philosophy. Giarretto slowly expanded the range of interventions from conjoint family therapy to a broad array of therapeutic tools to form the CSATP (Giarretto, 1978). From those beginnings, the CSATP has blossomed into a comprehensive treatment program that is frequently cited throughout the literature and that has become the model for other treatment programs throughout the United States.

In 1972, Giarretto and his wife Anna founded Parents United, a guided self-help group that is an essential element of the CSATP treatment program.

Program Goal

The goal of CSATP is "to resolve anger, hostility, shame, fear, and jealousy so that the people can communicate and function as a family again without incest" (Vander Mey & Neff, 1982, p. 727), and to "aim at healing the family, ridding involved persons of stigma, and maintain the family unit through re-educating the members and teaching them their various roles" (Vander Mey & Neff, 1982, pp. 727–728). Giarretto refers to treatment as a process of family resocialization (Giarretto, 1978, p. 184).

Treatment Components

Treatment modes include crisis intervention, counseling, and continuing support. Crisis intervention begins as soon as a report is filed disclosing the abuse. Often before the perpetrator is arrested, each parent receives a call from a Parents United peer counselor offering to make personal contact, share their mutual experience, and invite the parents to a Parents United meeting (Brecher, 1978, p. 28). The family and its members are then assessed for need and are offered a variety of social and community services designed to ease the immediate crisis touched off by the disclosure and report. Each family member is peer-supported through the adjudication process. With court/CSATP cooperation, the perpetrators are most often sentenced to an "open" community institution for three to six months, where they are able to keep their job, attend therapy and Parents United meetings, and return to the institution at night and on weekends. Consequently, they are able to retain their position as family provider, help pay the bills, keep the family financially stable, participate in treatment, and avoid the kind of family disruption experienced before CSATP was established (Brecher, 1978, p. 28). CSATP acknowledges the connection with the criminal justice system as being essential in motivating the offender to seek and remain in treatment: "The "shock effect" of legal intervention alters the whole situation and provides the needed base for family restructuring" (Brecher, 1978, p. 30). Counseling is provided around the objective of reconciling the victim–nonabusing parent relationship and then rebuilding the family around that core (Giarretto, 1976, pp. 64–65; Giarretto, 1978, pp. 215–216; Giarretto, 1982a, p. 273). In the course of developing the present program, it was determined that incest families are often too disorganized to respond effectively to immediate conjoint family therapy; therefore, various treatment modes are used to restructure the family to a point where conjoint therapy is possible. Those treatment modes are listed here, not necessarily in the order of importance or in the order of implementation in each case but, according to Giarretto, usually they are required in order to reconstitute the family:

- individual therapy (for the child victim, for the nonabusing parent, and for the abusing parent);
- victim–nonabusing parent therapy (eventually progressing to include all children in the family);
- marital therapy;
- perpetrator–victim therapy;
- family therapy; and
- group counseling and continuing support (Giarretto, 1976, 1978).

The period from crisis intervention and intake until the family is ready to join Parents United groups counseling is typically, but not limited to, nine months (Giarretto, 1982a, p. 273).

Treatment techniques include Gestalt therapy, enactment of critical scenes in the client's experience, use of directed behavior, fantasy, dreams, and bioenergetics (Giarretto, 1982b, pp. 228–239). Treatment focuses on:

- aiding the individual in recognizing and validating personal resources;
- forming new boundaries and intrafamily coalitions in order to facilitate family reconstruction;
- perpetrator accepting responsibility for the molestation and family acknowledgement and acceptance of responsibility, thereby freeing the child from responsibility; and
- review of marital relationship (Kroth, 1979, pp. 16, 17).

Individual and dyad counseling is provided by professional therapists, while group counseling is provided through Parents United and is facilitated by a combination of paid professionals, trained volunteers, and graduate interns. Continuing support is through affiliation with Parents United, which provides a variety of weekly peer group experiences such as: orientation groups, men's groups, women's groups, mixed gender groups, groups for women molested as children, social skills groups, and relationships groups (Giarretto, 1982b). Ongoing support is also available from Daughters and Sons United, an outgrowth of Parents United that offers counseling and support to the daughters and sons of abusers, and from groups such as Parents Anonymous (Vander Mey & Neff, 1982). Parents United and Daughters and Sons United groups are limited to five couples (or the equivalent) and are facilitated by staff members and trained Parents United member volunteers. Once a member completes a program of treatment, Parents United and Daughters and Sons United members may remain active as long as they choose. Members may eventually volunteer to become trained crisis interveners or group cofacilitators, thus moving from a role as an active member to a role as an active peer-supporter, public speaker, or public educator (Giarretto, 1982b).

Services

CSATP offers a variety of services to meet the needs of families during the initial crisis stage of intervention and throughout the treatment process. Among the services noted by Giarretto (1978, 1982b) are:

- Parents United member-volunteers provide support to new members in crisis consisting of babysitting, transportation, job referrals, and job training referrals.
- Parents United monitors legal fees for lawyers providing services to CSATP clients, makes referrals to lawyers with whom CSATP has had experience, and intervenes in legal matters when necessary.

- Information and referral services include hotline and referral services (crisis counseling and referrals); medical aid at a local hospital; legal services (referral to attorneys and/or Public Defender, community legal services for Civil or Juvenile Court, National Organization for Women for referrals to female attorneys); social and financial aid (DSS eligibility for General Assistance or AFDC, foster home placement, social casework services, DSS Protective Services casework, emergency food, and emergency clothing); housing (supervised, protected living through community facilities for spouse, child, family, group home for victims preparing to return to their family); employment (referrals for job and job training opportunities for any family member); and self-help (Parents United groups, Daughters and Sons United groups).

In addition, CSATP also offers training to outside entities wishing to establish CSATP-like programs, and a Community Awareness program that consists of three components: a Speakers Bureau, an Information Dispersal Service, and Media Coverage (Kroth, 1979, pp. 18–22).

Treatment Staff

The treatment staff consists of professionals, volunteers, and self-help group members (Giarretto, 1982b). Professionals are community workers specially trained by CSATP. Giarretto describes the professional staff as consisting of: a Program Administrator who, along with a Program Director, selects personnel, defines staff functions, screens volunteers, and coordinates program and human services and the criminal justice system; a Program Coordinator who screens referrals, assigns cases, and coordinates CSATP with the criminal justice system and human services agencies; an Administrative Assistant who maintains client files and data and supervises public speaking services; secretarial personnel; a Program Administrator who hires personnel, monitors the budget, and ensures compliance with federal, state, and local mandates; a Treatment and Training Director who designs and implements treatment and training programs and directs public information; and Counselors and Interns consisting of licensed Masters Degree holders with three to five years of experience in counseling (Giarretto, 1978, pp. 185–186; 1982b, pp. 20–21). No more recent description of staffing was found in the literature.

Clientele

The clientele are representative of the Santa Clara County area in which CSATP operates (Giarretto, 1976). Clients presenting for treatment include parents (mostly fathers) who have molested their children, children molested by parents, older siblings and extra-familial individuals, members of incest families, women molested as children, men molested as children, and individuals who molested children not related to them (Giarretto, 1978, p. 185). Giarretto describes them as predominantly white, middle class families with an average length of involvement of six months; the average age of child victims is ten or eleven years. Father–daughter incest occurred in 75 percent of the cases serviced (Giarretto, Giarretto, & Sgroi, 1985, p. 233). According to Giarretto, the CSATP clientele is similar in distribution to the racial composition of Santa Clara County: 76.8 percent white, 17.5 percent Hispanic, 3.0 percent Asian, 1.7 percent black, 1 percent other (Giarretto, 1978, p. 138). The workforce make-up of CSATP clientele is predominantly professional, semi-professional, and skilled blue-collar (Giarretto, 1978, p. 65). The median level of education is 12.5 years (Giarretto, 1978, p. 138). The program drop-out rate was estimated at 10 percent (Giarretto, 1978, p. 233). Six cases of recidivism were noted in families that did not complete treatment, but CSATP reports no cases of recidivism among any of the families receiving a minimum of ten hours of counseling before formal termination (Giarretto, 1978, p. 234).

Referrals come through the Police Department/Juvenile Probation Department (specially trained to investigate child abuse, neglect, and molestation), and from self-referring clients (Giarretto, 1978, p. 213).

Program Evaluation

CSATP is one of the few programs evaluated empirically. Prior to 1978, the success of treatment was based on staff evaluations of client and program progress. In 1978, the California State Director of Health appointed an independent investigator to evaluate the performance of CSATP: "The evaluator's overall conclusion is that the impact of CSATP family therapy in the treatment of intrafamilial child sexual abuse (incest) is positive, conclusive, and unmistakable!" (Giarretto, 1978 p. 225; 1982a, p. 275; Kroth, 1979). Measurements on forty-four separate indices of change were taken at three periods: intake (2–3 weeks of treatment), midterm (5.1 months of treatment), and near termination (14 months of treatment). Kroth's conclusion stated:

> From a statistical standpoint, 82 percent of the measures favored the family therapy approach and its efficacy, while 6 percent did not. Considering the proliferating case loads, the number of salaried counselors who carry out the therapeutic program, and the results of the study, the overall conclusion is that the impact of CSATP family therapy in the treatment of intrafamilial and child sexual abuse is positive and clear (Kroth, 1979, pp. 136, 137).

Giarretto evaluates the success of CSATP in terms of increased demand for service, percentage of families who are helped, recidivism, improved marital relationships, and the report of the Kroth investigation (Giarretto, Giarretto, & Sgroi, 1985, pp. 233–234; Giarretto, 1978; Giarretto, 1982b). Giarretto reports that the rate of referrals has increased substantially since 1971 and that a large number of families were being treated for a problem that has always plagued society but was previously ignored (Giarretto, 1982a, p. 275). Giarretto reports no known recidivism among more than six hundred families that received a minimum of ten hours of treatment before formal termination (Giarretto, 1978, p. 232). Giarretto reports that 90 percent of children in families fully completing treatment before termination were reunited with their families with less than 1 percent recidivism (Giarretto, 1982a, p. 264). Of success in improving the marital relationships of incest couples, Giarretto reports that as a result of the CSATP's policy of beginning counseling as quickly as possible after referral and continuing through successful termination, "far more" marriages were saved than before that policy was in place (Giarretto, 1978, p. 231). The report of the Evaluation Team of the California State Department of Health reported improvements such as: (1) children in treated families were able to return home sooner than children in untreated families; (2) decline in the duration and intensity of self-abusive behavior of victims; (3) improved psychological health and social functioning in treated victims; and (4) no recidivism in six hundred treated and terminated families. Overall recidivism rate is reported at .6 percent (Giarretto, 1978, p. 232; Kroth, 1979).

Parents United and Daughters and Sons United (PU/DSU)

While it is true that CSATP functions hand-in-glove with Parents United and Daughters and Sons United, PU/DSU can and does function autonomously. It seems worthwhile, then, to look at the various components of PU/DSU in the same manner we did CSATP. By doing so, distinctions between the two programs may become more clear.

Background

Parents United began in 1972 when Giarretto spontaneously asked a CSATP member to call a member of a family in which disclosure had just occurred and to offer a sympathetic ear and the benefit of her own experience. From that point on, peer support became an essential component of the CSATP. In June 1975, Parents United appointed a Board of Directors, developed bylaws, and incorporated as a nonprofit organization supported by the Rosenberg Foundation. Barry reports there were forty-six chapters in fifteen states in 1984 (Barry, 1984, p. 18). Giarretto reports the existence of eighty-nine Parents United chapters throughout the nation as of 1982 (Giarretto, 1982a, p. 268). From the original group a subgroup formed, Daughters United, a self-help group of teenage female victims and siblings of victims holding weekly meetings with options for play therapy, communications workshops, preadolescent groups for females, groups for adolescent females, and mixed adolescents groups. In addition to self-help and peer support, Daughters United, like Parents United, has strong community awareness and education components that prepare written and electronic media presentations. In 1978, Daughters United evolved to Daughters and Sons United to more overtly involve preadolescent and adolescent boys in CSATP programming. Since that expansion, there are DSU groups for boys wherever there is sufficient demand (Giarretto, 1978, pp. 206–211). DSU is governed by a six-member Task Force Committee that meets weekly with a PU Representative and DSU Coordinator. The committee establishes goals, objectives, and projects geared to enhance the development, organization, and unity of the DSU program. The committee assesses all new group formats and ensures that members who act as group facilitators with the professional group leaders are carefully selected and trained. DSU also organizes fundraising activities and administers the money collected. To build morale and *esprit de corps*, birthdays are celebrated and visits are arranged to entertainment and cultural centers (Giarretto, 1982b, p. 33). PU and DSU groups are facilitated by professional counselors and aided by graduate student interns (Kroth, 1978, p. 15).

Goal

The goal of PU is to provide a forum for shared experience and self-help for families who have experienced incest. As does the CSATP from which it evolved, PU seeks to provide a regenerative environment for resocialization, utilizing humanistic principles and working toward family healing, responsibility, and reunification (Giarretto, 1978; Sagatun, 1982, p. 99).

DSU is designed for children five to eighteen years old (primarily girls) who are victims or siblings of victims. Their goals are: to alleviate trauma in victims by providing emotional support; to facilitate awareness of feelings; to promote personal growth and communication skills; to alleviate guilt regarding the abuse; to prevent self-destructive behavior; to prevent repeated offense by increasing the victim's independence, assertiveness, and self-esteem; to prevent emotional/sexual dysfunction; and to break the multigenerational abusive and dysfunctional patterns (Giarretto, 1982a, p. 268; Giarretto, 1982b, p. 32).

PU Treatment Components

PU provides participants with exposure to a group process that gives clients an opportunity to compare their experience with that of peers, to increase self-direction and personal responsibility rather than dependence on professionals to be "cured," to learn positive social attitudes, and to increase confidence in their ability to cope with social problems (Giarretto, 1978, p. 205). Group counseling options are:

- preorientation groups for first time members (crisis-oriented);
- orientation groups for new members;
- men's groups;
- women's groups;
- groups for adults molested as children;
- human sexuality classes;
- couples' communication groups;
- open groups (e.g., general issues, communication skills);
- alcohol problem groups for present or former drinkers and those who relate to drinkers; and
- parenting groups.

Training is available for group leadership and sponsorship and peer counseling and for public speaking training for those interested in taking the CSATP philosophy and treatment concept into the public arena (Kroth, 1979, p. 15; Giarretto, 1982b, pp. 22–31).

DSU Treatment Components

DSU provides social and cultural activities and group experiences for children ages five to eighteen, such as:

- male offenders groups;
- play therapy for children;
- pre-adolescent groups;
- female adolescents groups;
- mixed adolescents groups;
- male adolescents groups;
- Making Life Happen Your Way (life planning and relationships for eighteen to twenty-five year olds);
- human sexuality classes; and
- Ten-week Communication Workshop (Kroth, 1979, p. 15; Giarretto, 1982b, pp. 31, 32).

Treatment is voluntary and cost free.

PU Services

Services offered to members through PU are largely provided on a member-to-member basis. These services include: babysitting, transportation, assistance with living arrangements, and one-on-one support. PU keeps a list of referrals for job possibilities, offers assistance in refreshing or building job skills, monitors legal assistance provider, invites speakers in to explain the services and functions of their agencies, maintains a list of companies willing to hire a parent with a felony record, uses its influence to help get work furloughs approved, and offers group counseling for members (Giarretto, 1978, pp. 206–209; Giarretto, 1982a, pp. 266–267). Group counseling services have already been described under the PU Treatment Components section.

DSU Services

A wide range of services is offered:

> A children's shelter liaison makes initial contact with a child who has been placed in a shelter within one or two days after admission in order to provide crisis intervention, introduce the child to DSU groups, and provide continual support and counseling throughout protective custody.

> A Juvenile Hall liaison performs the same function as the shelter liaison for children in Juvenile Hall.

> A home liaison makes initial contact during the crisis period with those children who remain in the home.

> Sponsorship Program members make telephone contacts with and facilitate new members' entry into the groups.

> A Time-Out Corner provides DSU members access to resources and reading materials that increase the children's knowledge in such areas as drug abuse, birth control, and communication skills.

> A support system for police and juvenile investigations, medical exams, and court hearings provides interns who accompany children through the various steps in the criminal justice system process.

> A Big Brother/Big Sister Unit provides interns who enter into one-on-one friendships with children requiring sustained support.

A transportation unit provides transportation for children to weekly groups and counseling sessions.

Community Awareness Presentations are offered by trained members.

DSU provides advocacy for children's rights (Giarretto, 1982b, pp. 32, 33).

Treatment Staff

According to Deaton and Sandlin (1980, p. 316), Parents United groups are facilitated by professional social workers and other therapists, and assisted by PU members who complete the sponsorship, leadership, and speakers' bureau training. Ongoing supervision is provided for trained PU facilitators as well as for the professional facilitators. Kroth reports that "each treatment group is facilitated by a professional counselor assisted by a graduate intern" (Kroth 1979, p. 15).

Clientele

No specific information is available at this time on the demographics of PU members. Because PU is a national organization, it is fair to speculate, while not confirmed in the literature, that the demographics of individual programs vary according to their geographic and physical location.

Program Evaluation

The only overall evaluation of PU was found in the Kroth (1978) independent evaluation of CSATP by the California State Department of Health. That report attributed success to PU based on measures of change in the victim, perpetrator, nonabusing parent, the marriage and family, and overall recidivism. The victim was reported to spend a median of ninety days out of the home, a figure much lower than reported before CSATP/PU began (Kroth, 1979), but not reported in any greater detail than what has just been related. Giarretto reported that 92 percent of female victims could be expected to return home eventually (Giarretto, 1982b, p. 52), again, a much lower figure than projected before CSATP/PU began, but no specifics were reported. Victims displaying nervous or psychosomatic symptoms at intake were described after treatment as "symptom free" in 94 percent of the sample. In 46 percent of victims, social skills were improved at treatment termination as compared with 4 percent in the intake sample. Improved victim–nonabusing parent and victim–nonabusing parent relationships were reported, along with reduction in the nervousness of nonmolested siblings from 18 percent to 12 percent (Bobrow, 1984). The perpetrator experienced shorter jail sentences and suspended sentences as a result of CSATP/PU treatment, and 89 percent of those sampled were ready to accept most or all responsibility for the molestation. Improvement in the self-esteem of perpetrators was also noted (Bobrow, 1984). The nonabusing parents in the sample reported reduction in strong feelings of guilt from 65 percent at intake to 24 percent at termination. At termination, 50 percent of the sample of nonabusing parents reported willingness to admit a high degree of responsibility for the molestation, compared with 0 percent at intake (Bobrow, 1984). Success in improvement in the marriage and family was determined by: (1) a decline in reports of nonexistent or declining sexual contact with each other among couples from 80 percent at intake to 24 percent at termination, and (2) a finding that 76 percent of couples in the sample remained together and were reconciled as a consequence of therapy. An additional 14 percent who had separated were still in therapy and had potential for reconciliation (Bobrow, 1984, p. 118). Self-reported improvement in the marital and family relationships were also noted (Giarretto, 1982b). Recidivism was reported between 2 and 20 percent. An average increase of 40 percent was noted in the numbers of clients coming forward each year—of which 98 percent are estimated by Kroth to be non-recidivists (Giarretto, 1982b, p. 55).

Alpha Human Services

All information for Alpha Human Services comes from *Retraining Adult Sex Offenders: Methods and Models* by Fay H. Knopp, for the Safer Society Program of the New York State Council of Churches. Knopp overviews sex offenders and treatment issues, and reviews ten treatment programs in the United States, of which Alpha Human Services is one. Recent conferral with Alpha Human Services confirms that, with minor modifications, the material in Knopp's book is still basically representative of the Alpha Program.

Background

Alpha Human Services Inc., in Minneapolis, Minnesota, opened in 1971 as a traditional halfway house for offenders leaving state prisons en route to rejoining the community. In 1973, it became totally treatment-oriented. In 1974, the program admitted its first sex offender. For several years following, sex offenders were only a small percentage of the treatment program's residents, but the numbers increased gradually until, in 1984, all of Alpha's residents were convicted sex offenders or had engaged in sexually offensive behavior. Originally, Alpha was a nonprofit agency funded by the U.S. Department of Justice's Law Enforcement Assistance Administration (LEAA), and later by the Minnesota Department of Corrections. As of 1984, when

Knopp gathered her information, Alpha functioned as a corporation, receiving no grant monies; rather, service was by contract with the referring agency and paid for by that agency, by the county, or by the individual who paid part or all of the costs. Treatment was cost-free once the client entered the postresidential phase of the program. Outpatient program costs were usually paid for by the client, by medical insurance, or by public funds.

Alpha serves thirty selected convicted sex offenders in addition to continuing treatment for a large number of postresidents who return to the house for group sessions, and other offenders who attend groups as part of the outpatient program. An experimental day program brings in a few convicted offenders who are still imprisoned to attend group and individual treatment sessions during a fourteen-hour day, returning to the correctional facility at night. A separate corporation provides occasional industry work project opportunities for the clients.

Program Goal

Based on the belief that most behavior is learned and that inappropriate behavior can therefore be replaced by appropriate behavior, the Alpha Human Services program emphasizes encouraging adaptive behavior in three basic areas: (1) developing and maintaining meaningful interpersonal relationships and family interaction (including appropriate sexual behavior), (2) developing and maintaining appropriate work-related behavior and ability to be self-supporting; and (3) developing and maintaining healthy and responsible community interaction. In order to successfully complete the program, a resident must have a high school diploma or GED and be working or in school full-time.

An implied secondary goal is to provide a nurturing family-like atmosphere in a noninstitutional setting where family roles and trust relationships can be experienced (maybe for the first time). According to Jane Matthews, former Alpha case supervisor and psychotherapist, "We try to let them know that we are coming from love, care and concern, rather than punitiveness or vindictiveness . . . we model care for others, and they learn that honesty does not have to be hurtful." Though highly structured, the "family" atmosphere attempts to supplement what many of the residents never had: ". . . a framework that people can grow in with consistent emotional support" (p. 131).

Treatment Components

The treatment program consists of four phases. The median for inpatient treatment is approximately eighteen months. Alpha projects eighteen months to two years of supervised oversight for inpatient clients.

Phase 1 can be accomplished in four to six months. For the first thirty days, the resident goes through a period of orientation, information gathering, and affirming the resident's commitment to treatment. The patient is assigned to routine work and maintenance responsibilities, becoming eligible for more responsible work assignments after thirty days of committed residence. Objectives of Phase I treatment are: (1) take full responsibility for the offense; (2) learn to process fantasies; (3) refrain from using early childhood experiences as excuses for your behavior; and (4) demonstrate real interaction with other program participants. These objectives are accomplished by working through the crime as both offender and victim, with the goal of helping the offender develop empathy and insight into the dynamics of the crime. Cognitive aversive conditioning helps to control and reshape deviant sexual fantasies. Work is done on developing concern and care for other people, even to the extent of bringing family members in for group sessions when indicated. During the first phase, privileges are kept to a minimum; privileges are earned as the resident begins to display trust, trustworthiness, and concern for others. Eventually conjugal visits may be earned.

Phase 2 is usually three to six months in duration, providing an opportunity to live out the learning accomplished in the first phase. The objective of Phase 2 is to work through the anger, fear, low self-esteem, and accumulated pain and desperation that are expressed sexually. Once offenders have learned alternate ways of dealing with pain and anxiety, they are encouraged to improve educationally through GED, vocational training, or another form of higher education in preparation for acquiring a job. Privileges such as leaving the house escorted or unescorted on a limited basis or participation in community activities can be earned as vocational improvements are made.

Phase 3 is a transitional phase, usually lasting three or four months. Work on therapeutic issues continues in preparation for a move to the community.

Phase 4, the postresidential phase, usually three to four months in duration, allows a former resident to live with spouse, family, a significant other, or another former resident in the community, while Alpha maintains legal oversight and monitoring. Eligibility is determined on a case-by-case basis. The objective of the fourth phase is to round out the offender's adaptability to independent life in the community. Once released, a former resident can return to Alpha for therapy and support or can use the 24-hour hotline.

Throughout treatment, both individual and group therapy is provided, supplemented by individual meetings with the case manager, case supervisor, marital counseling, and (in some cases) family therapy. Treatment is eclectic, favoring behavioral, affective, and cognitive techniques. Eleven scheduled two-hour groups meet weekly: three sexual behavior groups, one aggressive behavior group, a women's group, a couples' group, a privilege group, a general therapy group, a chemical use and abuse group, and two groups designed to meet specific needs of the residents at the time. Outside resources such as

Parents Anonymous and Planned Parenthood are brought in on an as-needed basis. Once a month there is a meeting for the entire treatment community. Unscheduled groups also meet: behavioral, emotive, and endorsement groups meet on an as-needed basis to confront and deal with specific situations or needs with the objective of getting to the underlying issues and working through them. Emotive groups encourage prompt and controlled expression of emotions. Endorsement groups provide positive feedback for a job well done or for exceptionally positive behavior.

Services

Services include

- marital counseling;
- family counseling;
- individual therapy;
- group therapy;
- human sexuality training;
- chemical abuse treatment;
- vocational and job readiness;
- community living readiness;
- 24-hour hotline;
- ongoing therapy and support;
- day treatment program;
- inpatient program; and
- outpatient program

Treatment Staff

The staff consists of an Executive Director, one licensed and degree-holding Program Coordinator/Case Supervisor, a Business Manager, an Intake Director, three degree-holding psychotherapists, one licensed psychologist Case Supervisor, three Case Managers, one full-time and several part-time night coordinators, a consulting psychiatrist, and a secretary. Alpha Service Industries has a staff that includes an Executive Director, a Business Manager, six psychotherapists (some of whom are also employed by the inpatient program), and a secretary shared by the inpatient program.

Clientele

Eligibility excludes active psychotic, brain-damaged, or intellectually defi-
cient persons. Most residents are classified as "character disordered." Eligible
clients must have incurred one conviction for a sexual offense; be available
for a minimum of eighteen months of treatment; parole or probation must
be contingent on successful completion of the Alpha program; and they must
be amenable to treatment. It must be established with confidence that the
prospective client is not likely to abscond, and if the client were to abscond,
must not constitute a serious threat to the safety of the community, must be
motivated to change, and must display an acceptable degree of impulse control. Referrals come from parole boards, probation officers, judges, or prison
caseworkers.

Based on figures provided in 1983, 78.3 percent of residents are white,
4.3 percent are Native American, 13 percent are black, and 4.3 percent are
Hispanic. Age of residents ranges from eighteen to forty or older with an
average age of thirty-three years. The modal age is thirty to thirty-nine years.
Educational level ranges from eleven years of education or less to one year
of college or more, with an average of twelve years of education. The educational mode was high school graduate or GED. Residents charged and convicted of a sexual offense constituted 82.6 percent, 4.3 percent were charged
and convicted of another offense, including assault, robbery, kidnapping, or
terroristic threats, and 13 percent were neither charged nor convicted, but
were referred for sexual problems. At program entry, 43.5 percent evidenced
no chemical dependency, 13 percent were alcohol dependent only, 34.8 percent were dually dependant, and 8.7 percent were classified "unknown." Juvenile records existed for 60.9 percent of clients. 56.5 percent of offenders
had no prior adult felony conviction, 43.5 percent had one or more adult
felony convictions. Problematic sexual behavior of all clients is described as
17.4 percent rape, 26.1 percent incest, 47.8 percent pedophilia, 4.3 percent
indecent liberties, and 4.3 percent other.

Program Evaluation

Knopp reports:

> Not one sex offender who has completed the program has been reconvicted
> of any felony, of any kind. In general, about 50 percent fail to complete the
> program. The majority either voluntarily leave the program or are adminis-
> tratively terminated. A few run away. For the first ten months of 1983, out
> of 16 terminations from the residential program, two persons absconded.
> Those administratively terminated usually fail repeatedly to comply with
> program rules, are not amenable to treatment, or threaten others. Those who
> voluntarily terminate usually believe that the jail or prison sentence facing

them is preferable to treatment, do not like the program, or claim that they do not need treatment. Often defendants claim to need and want treatment only as a ploy to obtain favorable plea agreements; later, they change their attitudes when they believe that they can spend less than a year in jail and be released without treatment. . . . Two convicted rapists committed new rape offenses while still in the program. One, a third-phase resident, committed his offense in 1976, and the other, a fourth-phase resident, committed his offense in 1977. However, no resident has been convicted of a felony since (Knopp, 1984, p. 143).

Alpha is designed primarily for the regressed, nonviolent offender. The repeat offenders described above were rapists. Alpha's experience seems to support the argument that violent offenders need to be confined in more secure facilities than nonviolent offenders. For us, assignment to a community-based facility would not be a viable treatment option for fixated or violent offenders until they had undergone extensive developmental and/or chemotherapy or other extensive therapy in conjunction with confinement in a correctional or mental health facility. One area of agreement between us is that there is no "acceptable risk" when dealing with sex offenders. We prefer to err on the side of caution.

We hope this review of two existing programs has given you some idea of what is available and some standard for imagining what is possible. People frequently ask us, "Why don't you start a treatment program? Grant money is out there if you look for it." We are not so sure there are hoards of people out there who want to grant funds to programs for treating perpetrators. There seems to be an implied equation between "treatment" and "helping." Who wants to help someone who commits sex offenses—especially against a child! We certainly are not *unwilling* to start a treatment program if we could find the money, the professional staff, a facility, and a community willing to accept such a service (none of which is a small undertaking). Who knows, maybe we will—or maybe you or your agency will!

7
Caring for the Caretaker

Needless to say, working with perpetrators is hard work. In fact, unless you are vigilant, it can be hazardous to your professional health! As is the case whenever we are working hard and fully involved, we can easily become drained. We all need to order our lives to keep our batteries charged. If we are to teach our clients how to take care of themselves, we need to model that caretaking by taking care of ourselves.
Suggestions for taking care of yourself:

1. **Read the published journal articles and books already on the market that deal with burnout and burnout prevention.** Follow the recommendations and suggestions these materials provide. Awareness is half the battle, but the other half is prevention and palliative intervention.

2. **It is essential that workers dealing with perpetrators have excellent supervision**—and lots of it. Included in supervision is access to psychologist and psychiatric backup. This work is too heavy to be done alone. Especially because perpetrators and their families spend a long period of time being dependent on the therapist or worker, the therapist or worker needs to have an objective star to steer by. It is easy to get drawn into the confusion of the client system. It is also easy when dealing with such emotional issues as these (especially if you are a victim of abuse) to be unaware of countertransference issues that interfere with the progress of the client. It is critical that you have an objective supervisor who can help clarify, advise, and keep you on track with the client system. Peer supervision is better than no supervision if no other arrangement is possible, but there is no substitute for quality super vision. If you can manage to scrape together whatever it costs, supervision, whether group supervision or individual supervision, is worth every dime.

3. **It is imperative that you *make time* for yourself.** There is a temptation to become overinvolved with dependent family systems such as these. They genuinely need you, but they also need to begin making their own decisions and taking responsibility for themselves. Make sure you are not accessible to your clients twenty-four hours a day. During periods of genuine crisis, get another worker to cover for you. The CPS worker, for example, may be

happy to exchange on-call status during periods of emergency, thereby giving you both some relief.

4. **Learn to play.** Not only do you need to treat yourself kindly while you are actively working, you need to get away from the work and do something that recreates you. Whether it be swimming, going to movies, tennis, needlework, shopping, recreational reading, or taking long walks, be sure to make time in your day to center yourself and keep things in perspective. A laugh wherever you can find one is therapeutic for the therapist. Getting out among people for a short brisk walk and a cup of hot coffee, whether alone or with a friend can help put things back into perspective. We do a lot of playing during worktime. Sometimes we manage to get a half hour together between clients. We might sit quietly together, but more than likely we have jokes or cartoons to swap, or "can you top this" stories to share. Lunch is a favorite time to loosen up, especially right after a group session. We spend a few moments debriefing, then business becomes off-limits for the remainder of the hour. Damn the glances of fellow diners: full speed ahead with a prescribed dose of well-earned frivolity. We have yet to be forcibly evicted from a restaurant, or forcibly admitted to a psychiatric center!

5. **Balance.** If there is a concept more crucial to therapy, we have yet to discover it. As human service workers, we are always helping clients to work toward a point of healthy balance in their lives. We need to practice what we preach. One way to balance your work with perpetrators is to make sure you have a number of other presenting problems on your caseload as well. We know professionals who find balance by working with adult victim survivors or with child victims. For us that feels lopsided. While we work with both victims and perpetrators, we also work with a variety of other clients. In addition we spend time speaking to public and private groups, teaching workshops, and instructing at the college level. We spend as much time as we can with friends and family. It can be very difficult to shift gears and let the people we love take care of us for a while, but an occasional weekend of being waited on by a willing mate, friend, or family member can be most restorative.

6. **Stay in touch with the professional community.** We make it a point to attend workshops when we can—not necessarily workshops on perpetrators or on sexual abuse. We try to keep our practice skills generalized enough that we are not limited to working with a narrow clientele. Therefore, we look for training workshops (especially those that necessitate leaving town for a day or two) that help broaden our practice skills. Aside from professional training, you can find some relief in keeping in touch with professional associates. Keeping in touch with other workers helps to reinforce your own sense of connection, purposefulness, achievement, and productivity.

7. **Stress management.** Working with perpetrators is stressful work. How do you assist your clients in dealing with stress? You might teach them relax-

ation exercises, creative visualization exercises, deep breathing, or biorhythm monitoring techniques. You might recommend physical exercise, developing hobbies, or planning and utilizing leisure time. These are all things you can do to manage your own stress. Physical exercise is an important part of any self-care program. Constructive expenditure of energy begets energy: run, jog, row, walk, play a racket sport or a team sport, but give yourself an opportunity to expend your stress-energy healthfully.

8. **Keep a journal.** Journal writing is not only therapeutic, it might also provide the material you will need when you add to the existing literature on treating perpetrators. Use your journal to keep in touch with your own re-actions to your work and your clients as well as for notes for a book or article.

Practice suggestions:

1. **Try to link the family with other resources and support services** so you are not single-handedly trying to help this family. Give them crisis intervention hotline numbers they can call when you are unavailable and they suddenly are overcome with an urgent need to talk to someone. If having an unlisted residential telephone number is a practical and comfortable option for you, we advise you to do that.

2. **Work closely with other involved professionals** (e.g., physicians, lawyers, the courts, CPS workers, police, DAs' offices, probation officers, etc.). Not only does professional cooperation keep you informed and up to date on other case developments, it fosters an interdisciplinary approach to case management and increases your professional support. Of course, you need to have signed releases all the way around in order to work this way, but that can be accomplished easily in most cases, and is of mutual benefit to everyone involved. We have found other professionals to be most receptive to this kind of cooperation. In our experience, it seems as though professionals instinctively understand the need for mutual support and assistance with this kind of case.

3. **About responsibility. . . .** It is important that you know that you are not responsible for healing this family or for solving their problems. Your involvement enables them to do some problem solving and to learn to deal with their own problems in the best way *they* can. Be careful not to "take the monkey on your back" or to make their problems yours. None of us can save all the people in the world who hurt. It is their choice to learn to deal with this crisis and to move beyond it or to stay immobilized. All you can do is to do your best to help the family cope and to protect the victim from revictimization. In the final analysis, each of us must live our own life and make our own decisions. If a client chooses to stay stuck, that is the client's choice, not your failure.

4. **Practice with someone you trust, respect, and enjoy.** If you are the only person in your office or agency working with perpetrators and their families,

find a support system—even if you have to construct one. We work in two locations: one is very rural, the other is suburban. In the suburban location we are lucky enough to have a specialized professional support group for those who work with adults abused as children. As it happens, many of the professionals also work with perpetrators, so the group supports those who work on that end of the problem as well. This group grew out of a fantastic lecture series initiated three years ago by the sponsoring agency. During that workshop/lecture series the need for such a group was identified, the professional community responded, and a few motivated people made tentative beginnings from which the present group has evolved. We meet on a designated day once a month for general support, to exchange information and materials, to hear speakers, to seek suggestions, and to share experiences. Even when we cannot get to meetings, we find it a comfort to know the group exists and is there for our support. What a difference from the rural community in which we have only each other! Neither of us can imagine practicing in total isolation.

Neither of us has a formula for burnout prevention, but we are glad to offer our experience in order to inform yours. In spite of all the positive things we have been suggesting (and we believe in them whole-heartedly), we have to admit to having times when we feel as though we are losing our minds. Those are the times when we need to remind ourselves to step back and regain our balance by using some of the suggestions we have shared with you. We all need to actively avoid allowing ourselves to get pulled into the crazy-making worlds of some of our clients.

We wish you well in your work and we hope that, in some way, sharing our experience helps make your work a little easier and a little more satisfying. The challenge is exceeded only by the need for workers such as yourselves who are willing to firmly, yet gently and respectfully, enter the chaotic lives of incestuous clients and try to help them create order.

We conclude with a salute to the courageous clients who want so much to change their lives that they allow people like us into them:

Dreams in Chains

Imprisoned by fear
Surfaced by need
Captured by guilt
Blocked by deception

Sensing the freedom of the soul
Only to climb to the top of the Euphoric
    mountain of circumstances
Is it chance? Or choice?

Control of the imaginary key that masters
   the magic combination for freedom.
Security in the confines of the darkened
   corridors of time.
Breathe the air of the endless universe
or consume the stagnated remains of
      a shattered past.
The chains are in my mind.

Carolyn Fuhrmann
1989.

References

After Conviction—The Adult Offender in Wisconsin. Madison, WI: League of Women Voters of Wisconsin, 1974.

Barry, R. J. "Incest: The last taboo." *F.B.I. Law Enforcement Bulletin,* January 1984, Vol. 53, No. 1, pp. 2–9; February 1984, Vol. 53, No. 2, pp. 15–19.

Bobrow, N. A., *Father-Daughter Incest: A Synthesis of the Literature on Theory and Treatment.* Ph.D. dissertation, Saint Louis University, University Microfilms International, 1984

Brecher, E. M. *Treatment Programs for Sex Offenders.* Department of Justice, Washington, D.C.: National Institute of Law Enforcement and Criminal Justice Prescriptive Package, U.S. Government Printing Office Stock Number 027–000–00591–8, January 1978.

Burgess, A. W., Groth, A. N., Holmstrom, L. L. & Sgroi, S. M. *Sexual Assault of Children and Adolescents.* Lexington, MA: Lexington Books, 1978.

Deaton, F. A. & Sandlin, D. L. "Sexual victimology within the home: A treatment approach." *Victimology: An International Journal,* 1980, Vol. 5, No. 2–4, pp. 311–321.

DeYoung, M. "Counterphobic behavior in multiply molested children." *Child Welfare,* 1984, Vol. LXIII, No. 4, pp. 333–339.

Forseth, L. B. & Brown, A. "Intrafamilial sexual abuse treatment centers." *Child Abuse and Neglect,* 1981, Vol. 5, pp. 177–186.

Giarretto, H. "A comprehensive child sexual abuse treatment program." *Child Abuse and Neglect,* 1982a, Vol. 6, pp. 263–278.

Giarretto, H. "Humanistic treatment of father-daughter incest." In Helfer, R. E. & Kemp, C. H. *Child Abuse and Neglect: The Family and the Community,* Cambridge, MA: Ballinger Publishing Co, 1976. Used by permission of Ballinger Division, Harper and Row Publishers, Inc.

Giarretto, H. *Integrated Treatment of Child Sexual Abuse: A Treatment and Training Manual.* Palo Alto, CA: Science and Behavior Books, 1982b.

Giarretto, H. *Integral Psychology in the Treatment of Father-Daughter Incest.* Ph.D. Dissertation. California Institute of Asian Studies, University Microfilms International, 1978.

Giarretto H., Giarretto M. & Sgroi S. M. "Coordinated community treatment of incest." In Burgess, A. W., Groth, A. N., Holmstrom, L. L. & Sgroi, S. M. *Sexual*

Assault of Children and Adolescents. Lexington, MA: Lexington Books, 1985, pp. 231–240.

Greer, J. G. & Stuart, I. R. *The Sexual Aggressor: Current Perspectives on Treatment.* New York: Van Nostrand Reinhold, 1983.

Groth, A. N. "Guidelines for the assessment and management of the offender." In Burgess, A. W. (ed). *Sexual Assault of Childen and Adolescents.* Lexington, MA: D. C. Heath & Co., 1978.

Groth, A. N. "The Incest Offender." In Sgroi, S. M. *Handbook of Clinical Intervention in Child Sexual Abuse.* Lexington, MA: D.C. Heath & Co., 1982.

Groth, A. N. Notes from lecture-workshop entitled *Child sexual abuse: Investigation and assessment of victims and offenders.* Sponsored by Forensic Mental Health Associates, Newton Center, Massachusetts. Buffalo, N. Y.: April 22 and 23, 1986.

Groth, A. N. & Birnbaum, H. J. *Men Who Rape: The Psychology of the Offender.* New York: Plenum Press, 1979.

Groth, A. N., Hobson, W. F. & Gary, T. S. "The child molester: Clinical observations." *Journal of Social Work and Human Sexuality,* Fall 1982, Vol. 1, pp. 129–144.

Groth, A. N., Longo, E. E. & McFadin, J. B. "Undetected recidivism among rapists and child molesters." *Crime and Delinquency,* July 1982, Vol. 28, No. 3, pp. 450–458.

Groth, A. N., et al. *Sexual Assault of Children and Adolescents* Lexington, MA: Lexington Books, 1978.

Helfer, R. "The War Cycle." In *The Diagnostic Process and Treatment Programs.* Washington, D.C.: U.S. Department of Health Education, Welfare, Office of Human Development Services, DHEW Publication No. OHDS 77–30069, 1977.

Herman, J. L. *Father-Daughter Incest.* Cambridge, MA: Harvard University Press, 1981.

Holmes, T. H. & Rahe, R. H. "Social readjustment rating scale." *Journal of Psychosomatic Research,* 1967, pp. 213–218.

Jeffers, S. *Feel the Fear and Do It Anyway.* New York: Harcourt Brace Jovanovich, 1987.

Kaufman, G. *Shame: The Power of Caring.* Cambridge, MA: Schenkman Books, 1980.

Knight, R. A., Schneider, B. E. & Rosenberg, R. "Classification of sexual offenders: Perspectives, methods, and validation." In *Rape and Sexual Assault: A Research Handbook* New York: Garland Publishing, 1985.

Knopp, F. H. *Retraining Adult Sex Offenders: Methods and Models.* Orwell, VT: Safer Society Press, 1984.

Kroth, J. A. *Child Sexual Abuse—Analysis of a Family Therapy Approach.* Springfield, IL: Charles C. Thomas, 1979.

Long, L. D. & Cope, C. S. "Curative factors in a male felony offender group." *Small Group Behavior,* November 1980, Vol. 11, No. 4, pp. 389–398.

MacDonald, G. J. & DiFuria, G. "A guided self help approach to the treatment of the habitual sex offender." *Hospital and Community Psychiatry,* October 1971, Vol. 22, No. 10, pp. 310–313.

Mayer, A. *Incest: A Treatment Manual for Therapy With Victims, Spouses and Offenders.* Holmes Beach, FL: Learning Publications, 1983.

Muenchow, A. & Slater, E. P. "Help for families coping with incest." *Practice Digest,* September 1978, Vol. 1, No. 2, pp. 18–22.

Pearman, W. A. "An empirical assessment of the public's view of retribution versus rehabilitation of criminal offenders." Association Paper, Pennsylvania Sociological Society. PA: SA Reproduction Service, 1983.

Puryear, D. A. *Helping People in Crisis.* (5th ed.) New York: Jossey-Bass Publishers, 1984.

Reid, W. H. "Pessimism and optimism in treating sex offenders." *The Psychiatric Times/Medicine & Behavior,* April 1988, pp. 8–11.

Sagatun, I. J. "Attributional effects of therapy with incestuous families." *Journal of Marital and Family Therapy,* January 1982, Vol. 8, No. 1, 99–104.

Sandhu, H. S. *Modern Corrections—The Offenders, Therapies, and Community Reintegration.* Springfield, IL: Charles C. Thomas, 1974.

Sanford, L. T. *The Silent Children.* New York: McGraw-Hill, 1982.

Schwartz, M. F. & Masters, W. H. "Treatment of paraphiliacs, pedophiles, and incest families." In Burgess, A. W. (ed.). *Rape and Sexual Assault: A Research Handbook.* New York: Garland Publishing, 1985, pp. 350–364.

Scritchlow, T. L. *Incest Parents: Their Personalities and the Effects of Treatment.* Ph.D. Dissertation, United States International University, University Microfilms International, 1982.

Sgroi, S. M. Notes from lecture-workshop entitled "Child sexual abuse: Investigation and assessment of victims and offenders." Sponsored by Forensic Mental Health Associates, Newton Center, Massachusetts. Buffalo, N. Y.: April 22 and 23, 1986.

Sgroi, S. M. *Handbook of Clinical Intervention in Child Sexual Abuse.* Lexington, MA: D.C. Heath & Co., 1982.

Silbert, M. & Pines, A. "Early sexual exploitation as an influence in prostitution." *Social Work,* 1983, Vol. 28, No. 4, pp. 285–289.

Simon, S. & Simon, S. Workshop and lecture notes entitled "Forgiveness: The essential passage to wellness and maturity." Rochester, N. Y.: Roberts Wesleyan College, March 13–14, 1987.

State of New York Penal Law, Article 263, Part 3. "Sexual performance by a child." Binghamton, N. Y.: Gould Publications, 1989–90.

Taubman, S. "Incest in context." *Social Work,* January–February 1984, Vol. 29, No. 1, pp. 35–40.

Taylor, R. L. "Marital therapy in the treatment of incest." *Social Casework,* April 1984, Vol. 65, No. 4, pp. 195–202.

Too Young to Run: The Status of Child Abuse in America. Washington, D.C.: Child Welfare League of America, 1986.

Vander Mey, B. J. & Neff, R. L. "Adult-child incest: A review of research and treatment." *Adolescence,* Winter 1982, Vol XVII, No. 68, pp. 717–735.

"Why, God—Why me?" Video tape by Varied Directions, Inc. 69 Elm Street, Camden, Maine 04843, (207) 236–8506, Fax (207) 236–4512.

Wise, M. L. From workshop observations and lecture notes: "Victim-survivor paradox: Therapeutic needs and process for adults who were sexually abused as children." Rochester, N. Y.: September 26–27, 1985.

Index

Desensitization therapy, 86
Developmental therapy issues, 19, 20
*Diagnostic Process and Treatment
Programs* (Helfer), 26
Diaries, 69. *See also* Journal writing
Drieblatt, Irwin, 97, 104
Drug use, 103; abuse programs, 88–89,
91; by sexual abuse victims, 2, 36,
42
Drug therapy, 84–86, 105

Education: of perpetrators, 123–124;
of public, 91, 106
Elder abuse, 3, 83, 128
Emotional abuse, 5, 26, 88–89
"Empirical Assessment of the Public's
View of Retribution Versus
Rehabilitation of Criminal
Offenders, An" (Pearman), 79
Empowerment, 48–49
Empty chair therapy technique, 68

Family: abuse and, 15, 26, 61, 88–89,
102; control in, 31–32;
dysfunctional, 111, 118; fortress
concept, 31–32, 102, 114;
reintegration of offender into, 80–
81, 82, 85, 86–89, 92, 95, 101, 106,
107; role reversal in, 26; secret
concept, 114–115, 120; therapy,
15–16, 24, 30, 39, 67, 77, 79, 80,
82, 85, 86–89, 93, 100–101, 107,
111, 147
Family Court, 90, 97
Fantasies, deviant, 104
Feel the Fear and Do It Anyway
(Jeffers), 48
Festinger, Leon, 45
FIRO (Fundamental Interpersonal
Relationship Orientation) Awareness
Scales, 96, 106, 125, 129–131, 135,
138, 141
Fixated offenders, 14; characteristics
of, 16–19, 102; continued offense
risk and, 21. *See also* Recidivism.
defined, 15, 16; drug therapy for,
84; example of, 25–26;
reintegration of, 23; same-sex
orientation, 18, 20; treatment of,
19, 20, 22
Forgiveness, 57–66, 67, 80

Freeman-Longo, Robert, 99–100
Freud, Sigmund, 15

Gary, T. S., 106
Gestalt therapy, 75, 147
Giarretto, Anna, 146
Giarretto, Henry, 136, 146, 148, 149,
150–152
Greer, Joanne, 86
Groth, A. Nicholas, 81, 106; on drug
therapy, 84, 85; on recidivism, 94–
96; on reporting requirements, 98;
on sentencing politics, 99, 100,
102–103; on treatment options, 81,
83, 86, 89, 90, 103; typology of
offenders, 11, 14, 15–20, 24, 53,
77, 79, 82, 100, 101
Group treatment, 82, 83–84, 89, 90–
91, 142–143, 147; model, 113–124;
sample program proposal, 127–134;
sample research design proposal,
134–142; starting strategies, 124–
126; termination of, 124
"Guidelines for the Assessment and
Management of the Offender"
(Groth), 20, 95–96
Guilt: admission of, 34; and
sentencing, 99; of victim, 1, 42, 44,
122

Halfway houses, 83, 87, 89–90, 91,
156
*Handbook of Clinical Intervention in
Child Sexual Abuse* (Sgroi), 12, 82,
85, 89, 96, 102
Hebephilia, 20
Helfer, Ray, 11, 26–29. *See also*
W.A.R. (World of Abnormal
Rearing) Cycle
Heterosexual Skills Retraining, 86
Hobson, W. F., 106
Holmes, T. H., 53
Holmstrom, L. L., 96
Homicide threats, 98
Homosexuality, 16, 18, 20
Hoyt/Goodhue bill, 97
Human service workers: case
management responsibilities, 89;
crisis intervention and, 32–40;
guidelines for, 163–166; relationship
to perpetrators, 5–6, 38; as role

About the Authors

Sandra Ingersoll (M.S.C., Canisus College) has a varied history of experience in the human services field. She has been employed as a social worker, a college instructor, and a counselor in private practice. Her volunteer experience has included individual and group counseling for Parents Anonymous of Buffalo and the Caring Coalition of Western New York; planning, policy development, and legislative development with the Chautauqua County Sexual Abuse Task Force; and facilitating therapy groups for incarcerated sex offenders in a New York State correctional facility. She is a popular speaker in her community and in surrounding communities. Currently, she is Director of Residential Maternity Services for Our Lady of Victory Infant Home in Lackawanna (Buffalo), New York. Her experience has put her in direct contact with all aspects of intrafamilial sexual abuse: victims, nonvictimized family members, extended family members, and victimizers. She has worked therapeutically with clients individually, in groups, in private practice, in prison settings, through agencies, hospitals, and institutions. This book flows from her therapeutic experience with perpetrators of sex crimes, which was in turn inspired by her interest in, experience with, and empathy for victims of sex crimes.

    Susan Patton (M.S.W., SUNY-Buffalo Graduate School of Social Work) is licensed and certified by New York State for the practice of social work. Susan's experience in human services began after raising a family. She has been employed as a secretary, a college instructor, a counselor in private practice, a social caseworker, and an Employee Assistance Program counselor. In volunteer capacities, she has done outreach work, taught, prepared and presented workshops for professional and community groups; designed and facilitated therapeutic groups for victims, co-facilitated therapeutic groups for incarcerated sex offenders in New York State correctional facilities; and served on community committees and boards of directors. She is a member of the National Association of Social Workers, the Monroe County Counselors Association, and the Victim-Survivor Professional Network. Currently, Susan is a Senior Counselor with the Employee Assistance Program of the

Health Association of Rochester and Monroe County, Inc., maintains a limited private practice, and teaches human service courses to incarcerated students through Medaille College. Susan's interest in perpetrator treatment began as work with victims of sexual abuse and their families. While attempting to adjust to the overwhelming number of victims presenting for therapy services, she became acutely aware of the trauma incurred when untreated or treated-and-released perpetrators maintain proximity to the victim and family, often victimizing or revictimizing other family members. While she has come to see perpetrators as individuals with severe social and personal dysfunctions, she never loses sight of the need to treat the victimizer in order to protect the child victim, potential victims, and family members.